THE

CAVALIER KING CHARLES SPANIEL

IN NORTH AMERICA

Barbara Garnett-Smith

with illustrations by
Betty Turner, Michael Allen and Barb Hoorman

CASCADE

PUBLICATIONS

The Cavalier's Pets by Sir Edwin Landseer. Reproduction courtesy Tate Gallery, London.

Buy a pup and your money will buy

Love unflinching that cannot lie.

Perfect passion and worship fed

By a kick in the ribs or a pat on the head.

Nevertheless it is hardly fair

To risk your heart for a dog to tear.

Rudyard Kipling

The Cavalier King Charles Spaniel in North America

Copyright 1998 by Barbara Garnett-Smith

ISBN 0-9662985-0-0

Cataloging in Publication Data

Many manufacturers secure trademark rights for their products. When Cascade Publications is aware of a trademark claim, we print the product name as trademarked or in initial capital letters.

Cascade Publications accepts no responsibility for veterinary medical information, suggested treatments or vaccinations mentioned herein. The reader is advised to check with their local, licensed veterinarain if at all possible before giving medical attention.

This book is available at special quantity discounts for breeders and clubs for promotions, premiums, or educational use. Write for details.

Front Cover: Ch. Grantilley English Rose at Laughing. Photo by Michael Allen. Back Cover: Benchmark Bunny Hop. Photo by Leon, Moto Photo.

Design and layout: Barb Hoorman.

1 2 3 4 5 6 7 8 9 0

Printed in the United States of America.

TABLE OF CONTENTS

DEDICATION

*In loving memory of
my husband, Bob*

ACKNOWLEDGEMENTS

Thank you to:

Elaine Mitchell for her immeasurable help throughout the book,
especially with the chapters on training, grooming and showing;

Betty Turner for the drawings for the chapter headings;

Michael Allen for the illustrations of the Breed Standard;

Many friends who generously gave their help and support;

My brother *Peter Garnett* and my dear friend *Barb Hoorman*,
without whom I would have never finished this project.

Three of the author's successful imports. CKCSC, USA and AKC Champion Grantilley English Rose at Laughing (top left), International, French, Dutch, Luxembourg, Belgian, Canadian, AKC and Reserve World Champion Hewshia Des Marliviers at Laughing (top right) and English, Canadian and CKCSC, USA Champion Alansmere Rhett Butler (bottom).

ABOUT THE AUTHOR

The author, Barbara Garnett-Smith with her late husband Bob and the 1992 CKCSC National Specialty winner Champion Laughing Charisma.

Barbara Garnett-Smith was born in Cheltenham, England, and attended school in Canada and university in France. She moved to the United States in 1965 and married in 1969. Barbara and her husband lived in San Francisco and exhibited Arabian horses before "going to the dogs" in the late 1970's.

Although Barbara's family in England had owned Cavaliers for many years, it was not until one of her aunts surprised her and her husband with a puppy as a gift that their involvement with Cavaliers began. Soon, another Cavalier followed the first, and Laughing Cavaliers was established.

Over the past twenty years, Laughing Cavaliers has imported some remarkable Cavaliers from England and Europe. These Cavaliers and their progeny have produced a number of Canadian, AKC and CKCSC, USA champions, including a National Specialty winner, a Reserve National Specialty winner, and the first Cavalier to win Best of Breed at the prestigious Westminster Kennel Club Show.

A Cavalier breeder—judge and exhibitor, Barbara lives with Cavaliers of all ages on a ranch located near Mount Hood, Oregon.

FOREWORD

When I heard that the Cavalier King Charles Spaniel was soon to be accepted by The American Kennel Club (AKC), I wondered how long it would be before someone would write a new book on the breed in the United States. I was delighted when I heard that the author of such a book was to be Barbara Garnett-Smith. She has been in the breed for some time and has worked hard to bring it to a high standard. She has imported some of the best blood-lines from England in order to improve the Cavalier in the United States (not a very easy thing to do when the breed is comparatively unknown to members of the public).

Until 1973, the Cavalier in England was one of the best-kept secrets. That year, a Cavalier became the first Toy Group winner to go Best in Show at the world-famous Crufts Dog Show. The dog was called Alansmere Aquarius, and he was just seventeen months old! Because he was seen world-wide on television and in all the international papers and magazines, Cavaliers took off almost over-night. Cavaliers in America will have a much higher profile now that the general public can see them at AKC shows, and it will be no surprise to people like me when they take to our charming and delightful dogs. There will be many problems for the American breeders, who have been moving along very slowly for many years. Many unscrupulous dealers will try to get in on the ground floor to try to make a fast buck. This happened in England back in 1973, but we were lucky enough to have a band of strong-minded breeders who stuck it out against all odds. I am sure that the same thing will happen in the United States. Breeders will have to go through this in order to come out on the other side with a much stronger and more established breed.

I hope that this book will help to protect the Cavalier King Charles Spaniel and guide new breeders down the right path. A dog breeder is someone who spends all his or her time working with the dogs, cleaning out kennels and sitting up all night whelping bitches. To change into a writer, means putting down on a blank sheet of paper everything that you do evey day as a breeder which is not easy. I have done this myself, and I know how difficult it is, but when the book is finished and a person says to you how helpful it is, then it is all worthwhile.

John Evans,
Alansmere Cavalier King Charles Spaniels,
June 30, 1996

Author of <u>The Cavalier King Charles Spaniel, An Owner's Companion.</u>

John Evans (right) with Alan Hall (left), and their record breaking Cavalier, English Champion Spring Tide of Alansmere.

. .10. .

INTRODUCTION

My involvement with Cavalier King Charles Spaniels began with a visit in 1977 to one of my aunts in England, who owned a wonderfully quaint fourteenth century pub in the village of Castle Combe, Wiltshire. Life in the pub revolved around Tiger, her beer-loving Cavalier, who lavished his attentions on those who would buy him a pint of his favorite brew. Tiger was the first Cavalier that I met, and I didn't realize that he was typical of the breed—mischievous, endearing and affectionate.

Six months after my return to San Francisco, an unexpected call from British Airways sent my husband Bob and me to the airport. Filled with curiosity, we went to the air-freight office, where to our delight, a diminutive version of Tiger was waiting—a gift from my aunt. Thus began our love affair with this wonderful breed.

Cavalier King Charles Spaniels are a rare combination of lap dog and sporting dog. They have been bred for centuries to be companions and subsequently have an intrinsic love of mankind. Cavaliers, as the largest member of the Toy Group, are an ideal size. They are small, yet large enough to please even those who shy away from diminutive toy breeds.

The number of Cavaliers in North America has increased dramatically in the past decade. Their popularity on both sides of the border surged in the mid-1980's when President and Mrs. Ronald Reagan were joined in the White House by an irrepressible Cavalier named Rex. With the recent recognition of the Cavalier by the American Kennel Club (AKC), popularity will continue to soar. Those who are devoted to the breed have a tremendous responsibility to see that the Cavalier is not ruined by commercialization and exploitation.

When people call for information about Cavaliers, I tend to get carried away extolling their virtues. I can almost hear the person on the other end of the phone thinking: "What a line!" What I tell them is no line—Cavaliers are everything that they are reputed to be and even more.

Tiger enjoying his pint of brew.

Portrait of a Lady. Dutch Seventeenth Century by Gabriel Metsu.
Reproduction courtesy The Minneapolis Institute of Fine Arts, Minneapolis, Minnesota.

chapter one
HISTORY OF THE BREED

The Earliest Cavaliers

The history of the Cavalier King Charles Spaniel and the English Toy Spaniel (King Charles Spaniel) is the same for several centuries, and a fascinating history it is. Spaniels of the Cavalier type are to be seen in many paintings by Europe's Old Masters of the fifteenth to nineteenth centuries, including Gainsborough, Landseer, Reynolds, Stubbs, Metsu, Titian, and Van Dyke. While the actual origin of the dogs is unknown, Titian's 1477 painting of the Venetian Duchess of Urbino with her small red-and-white spaniel is the first evidence of their existence. Yet it is with English royalty that they are most frequently associated. According to historians, the only dogs that King Henry VIII would allow at his court were "some small spaniels for the ladies." An intriguing suggestion is that King Henry's fourth wife, the Flemish Anne of Cleeves, may have brought the black and white Holland Spaniel with her to England, a likely ancestor of today's tricolor. The first visual record of the breed with English royalty is Antonio Moro's 1554 painting of two small spaniels lying at the feet of King Henry's daughter, Queen Mary I, and her husband Philip.

Dr. Johannes Caius, the personal physician to Queen Elizabeth I, wrote a dissertation in 1570 titled <u>De Canibus Britanicus,</u> in which all known dogs of the period were classified into groups. In this discourse, the small spaniels were referred to as the "Spaniel gentle or comforter: a delicate, neat and pretty kind of dog." The title of comforter was an earned one, as not only were the dogs placed under ladies' voluminous skirts for foot warmers and held close to the body during long carriage rides for warmth, it was also believed that they could cure stomach ailments and other diseases. In a time before flea control, they had the job of keeping biting pests away from their masters and mistresses.

The "spaniel gentle" played a role in gorier parts of history, accompanying both a Scottish and an English monarch to their execution. The official account of the beheading of Mary, Queen of Scots at Fotheringay Castle in 1549 read: "Then one of the executioners, pulling off her garters, espied her little dog which was

Mary Stewart by Nicholas Maes. Reproduction courtesy The Putnam Foundation, Timken Museum of Art, San Diego, CA.

Blenheim King Charles Spaniel in a Landscape.
18th Century English School, Attributed to Philip Reinagle.
Reproduction Courtesy Sara Davenport Fine Paintings, London.

crept under her clothes which could not be gotten forth but by force, yet afterwards would not depart from the dead corpse, but came and lay between her head and her shoulders, which being imbued with her blood, was carried away and washed." The little dog died two days late, supposedly of grief. In 1648, the ill-fated Mary Queen of Scots grandson King Charles I was also beheaded for treason, and he too was reportedly accompanied to the gallows by his small spaniel, who was later taken away and exhibited in London.

The execution of Charles I marked the beginning of England's short-lived experiment with republicanism, during which time the royal family was exiled to France. When Charles II, the son of the executed King Charles I, was restored to the English throne in 1660, the celebrated diarist Samuel Pepys noted that Charles returned to England accompanied by his favorite spaniel. Pepys complained sourly that he was given the task of "escorting the dog the King loved and his footman into a small boat to be rowed ashore."

The little dogs were everywhere the king went—in the council rooms, in the king's bedchamber, and even in church. Legend says that by royal decree they were allowed to enter any law court and to travel free on any public transport in the kingdom, although the authenticity of this legend has never been proven. Samuel Pepys grumbled in his diary, "All I observed was the silliness of the King playing with his dogs all the while and not minding the business," and he often wrote vitriolic critiques in his journal. Another diarist of the time, John Evelyn, noted "The king took delight in having a number of little spaniels follow him and lie in his bed chamber which

King Charles Spaniel. Nineteenth Century English School. Reproduction courtesy The William Secord Gallery, Inc., New York, NY.

. . 14 . .

rendered it offensive and indeed, the whole court was nasty and stinking." For anti-royalists, the dogs became symbols of royal inefficiency. Lord Rochester, one of the contemporary court wits, wrote:

"In all affairs of Church and State
He very zealous is and able
Devout at prayers and sits up late
At the Cabal or Council Table
His very dog at Council Board
Sits grave and wise as any Lord."

To the general public, Charles and his spaniel companions were very popular. Macaulay's History of England contains an account of Charles that reads: "He might be seen before the dew was off the grass in St. James' Park, striding through the trees, playing with his spaniels and flinging corn to his ducks, and these exhibitions endeared him to the common people, who always like to see the great unbend."

King Charles Spaniel. Nineteenth Century English School. Reproduction courtesy The William Secord Gallery, Inc., New York, NY.

Probably due to the fact that they had become such a favorite of the wealthy, the dogs began to be kidnapped for ransom. This led to many heartrending requests for the return of a beloved companion, which can be seen to this day in the archives of the London Gazette.

When Charles' favorite sister, Henrietta Stewart left England to marry Monsieur, the Dauphin of France, she took some of her spaniels with her to her new home. A portrait by Mignard painted in 1665 shows her with a tiny red-and-white spaniel with a flat skull and large eyes. After Henrietta's untimely death from suspected poisoning, her lady-in-waiting, Louise de Kerouaille (who was later to become Charles' mistress), fled back to England, accompanied by what were believed to be Henrietta's dogs.

While King Charles lay on his death-bed, he apologized for the length of time he was taking to die, but insisted that his spaniels remain by his side, much to the chagrin of the attending clergy. It is hardly surprising that the dogs were eventually given the name of their beloved master.

When Charles brother James became king, he continued the tradition of having the little dogs of the Cavalier type in the palace and it was not until his daughter Mary and her husband Wiliam of Orange came to the throne in 1689 that the look of the spaniel so loved by the Stuart kings began to change. In days gone by, the tastes of the royal court set the fashion trend, and the fancy of King

Amerglow Mimosa Rose—"Minnie Mouse," a King Charles Spaniel owned by Pat Wells. Photo by Meager.

The Cavalier King Charles Spaniel as depicted by artist George Stubbs for the Britsih Royal Mail Stamps. Courtesy of Royal Mail Stamps, England.

William and Queen Mary for the Chinese Pug led to a widespread vogue for the flatter-faced breeds. Gradually the look of the pretty little spaniel with the finer muzzle began to alter.

In the late 1600's King William made John Churchill the Duke of Marlborough, in appreciation of his distinguished military service. The Churchill's were great dog lovers, and they developed a unique dog that was known as the "Marlborough Spaniel", known for its happy temperament and sporting instinct. When The War of Spanish Succession broke out in the early 1700's, the Duke led the British army to victory in several major battles, one of which was the Battle of Blenheim. In gratitude, the British government built a palace for the Churchills on their Marlborough estate, and named it "Blenheim" in commemoration of the Duke's triumph. It was thus that the red-and-white Marlborough Spaniel came to be known as Blenheim. These dogs are among the ancestors of today's Cavaliers.

There is a charming legend about Sarah, the Duchess of Marlborough, that tells of her anxiously waiting at home for news of the outcome of the Battle of Blenheim. It is said that while waiting, the Duchess spent much time stroking the head of one of her red -and- white bitches who was heavily in-whelp at the time. Soon after, five puppies were born, all of which bore the Duchess' thumb print on top of their heads. From that time on, it was particularly desirable for the spaniels of the red- and -white color to bear this thumb print, which is known today as the "Blenheim spot" or lozenge.

During the 1700's, the gentleman's sporting artist, George Stubbs often featured Cavaliers in his paintings. In 1991, the Royal Mail issued a set of dog stamps commemorating his work. The Cavalier depicted shows remarkable resemblance to the modern day Cavalier.

Queen Victoria received her beloved tricolor spaniel "Dash" as a gift in 1833, when she was fifteen years old. Dash was certainly of the Cavalier-type, which can be seen in the often copied famous needlework picture of him. Sidney Lee in the Ladies Kennel Journal of 1896 reported this about Victoria on her coronation day in 1838: "Despite her consciousness of the responsibilities of her station, the Queen still had much of the child's lightness and simplicity of heart. On returning to the Palace she hastily doffed her splendors in order to give her pet spaniel Dash its afternoon bath." A memorial stone to Dash stands in the gardens of Adelaide Lodge showing his death at nine years of age, on December 20, 1842.

In the mid-1800's, the "nosey" form of Cavaliers began to disappear completely, soon to be replaced by the short-nosed King Charles Spaniel. In 1849 an article in The Field read: "The King Charles and Blenheim Spaniels as bred by the fancy, are snub-nosed, round-headed animals like Pugs, with silky ears and coats, but they are truly graceful animals. In Joyce Birchall's King Charles Spaniels she states "it is considered generally that a bull-dog cross gave the flat face; some, however, contend this was due to the Pug or Japanese crossing." The small spaniels with the longer nose, so popular with the Stuart Kings soon disappeared.

The Original Type Is Reborn

It was an American who was responsible for the resurrection of the breed as it looked in the time of King Charles II. In 1926, wealthy Roswell Eldridge of New York went to England hoping to purchase a pair of the old type of spaniels that he remembered from paintings seen in his childhood.

Gertrude Brown Albrecht, the guardian of the Breed in the early years of the CKCSC, USA.

not register her dogs with the American Kennel Club, because the breed was not recognized at that time. Therefore, she set out to contact any owners whom she could find on this side of the Atlantic, which at that time numbered less than a dozen. She established an active little nucleus of Cavalier enthusiasts among her family and friends in the Louisville, Kentucky area and in 1954 founded the Cavalier King Charles Spaniel Club, USA (CKCSC, USA), the official breed club and only registering body for Cavaliers in the United States for almost half a decade. Originally begun as an American chapter of the English Cavalier Club, the existence of the Cavalier King Charles Spaniel Club, USA, is directly attributable to Sally Brown's steadfast efforts in creating a stud book and her tireless work to establish the fledgling club. Incorporation took place in 1956, with Sally Brown serving as the club's president until 1962.

It is Mrs. Brown's sister-in-law, Gertrude Polk Brown, who is nevertheless the acknowledged guardian of the breed in the United States. Trudy Brown was the enthusiastic owner of a puppy from the first litter born to Sally Brown's bitch, Mercury of Eyeworth. After ten years of unyielding efforts to create a solid club and an impeccable stud book, Sally Brown handed over the reins to her sister-in-law, who became its guiding spirit. Trudy's husband, George Garvin Brown, died in the early 1970s, and several years later she married Jay Albrecht. The death of Trudy Brown Albrecht in 1983 was greatly mourned by all Cavalier enthusiasts.

Another influential person in the early

Alice Warden with judge Ann Rogers Clark winning
Best in Show with Homerbrent Mickey Finn at the Cavalier King
Charles Spaniel Club, USA National Specialty, May 1975.
Photo by Bud Warden.

Mary Rose Jepsky with Gertrude Brown Albrecht. Homerbrent
Monaveen is shown winning the George Garvin Brown
Memorial Trophy, 1975 CKCSC, USA National Specialty.
Photo by Glover.

years of the breed in the United States was Elizabeth Spalding. Working with Sally and Trudy Brown in the club's formative years, Miss Spalding also was an exhibitor at club shows, where her dogs were consistent winners. Miss Spalding owned Pargeter Lotus of Kilspindie, who won Best in Show at the first National Specialty in 1962, as well as Pargeter Mermaid, Reserve Best in Show and Best Opposite Sex at that same show. This first specialty show had fourteen dogs and twenty-one bitches entered—seventeen Blenheims, eight tricolors, four rubies and six black and tans—for a total number of twenty-six exhibitors, a far cry from the numbers exhibited today.

Early on, the CKCSC, USA applied to the AKC for Miscellaneous status, which was granted in 1962. After several applications by the club to gain full recognition were rejected by the AKC, the CKCSC, USA proceeded to go about its own business. A show system was developed and a stringent code of ethics was adopted. Although few Cavaliers were exhibited in the Miscellaneous classes, CKCSC, USA members did participate in and enjoy AKC obedience events. In 1962, Elizabeth Spalding was the first to complete AKC Companion Dog obedience titles on Miss Eda of

Manscross and Kingfisher of Kilspindie.

The CKCSC, USA membership was polled on numerous occasions over the years regarding full recognition, but they felt that the club's strictly enforced, stringent code of ethics afforded the breed a protective umbrella, precluding it from being commercially bred. They had as an example the enormous rise in popularity of the breed in England after Alansmere Aquarius won Best in Show at Crufts in 1973. The vote for full recognition was defeated by a large margin each time it was put to the membership, although Miscellaneous status was retained for obedience enthusiasts.

In 1992, the CKCSC, USA was invited by the AKC to become its parent club for the Cavalier King Charles Spaniel, but the membership voted nine to one against accepting the AKC's invitation to affiliate. A small group of CKCSC, USA members formed the American Cavalier King Charles Spaniel Club (ACKCSC), and they applied to the AKC for parent-club status. This was granted, and in March 1995, the breed was officially recognized by the AKC. The CKCSC, USA continues to operate as an independent breed registry with its own specialty-show system, while the ACKCSC became the parent club for the breed within the AKC. Cavaliers went into competition in the Toy Group in the AKC as of January 1, 1996. The ACKCSC held its first National Specialty in May 1997, with Best of Breed going to AKC Ch. Ravenrush Impresario, owned by Cynthia Madden.

January 1997 saw a historic first for Cavaliers when CKCSC, USA and AKC Ch. Partridge Wood Laughing Misdemeanour, owned by Cindy Lazzeroni, won Best of Breed and a Toy Group placement at the prestigious Westminster Kennel Club show.

The long-term effect of AKC recognition of the breed in the United States is yet to be determined, but one thing is certain—The Cavalier King Charles Spaniel will continue to be protected by those in both old clubs and new, who are truly dedicated to its preservation.

*National Specialty Winners, Cavalier King Charles Spaniel Club, USA 1962 — 1997**

1962 *Pargeter Lotus of Kilspindie*
Owner: Elizabeth Spalding
Breeder: Mrs. B. Keswick, England
Blenheim Dog

1963 *Pargeter Mermaid*
Owner: Elizabeth Spalding
Breeder: Mrs. B. Keswick, England
Blenheim Bitch

1964 *Pandora of Dendy*
Owner: Mrs. Garvin Brown
Breeder: Beryl Sadler, England
Blenheim Bitch

1965 *Pandora of Dendy*
Owner: Mrs. Garvin Brown
Breeder: Beryl Sadler, England
Blenheim Bitch

1966 *Pargeter Waggoner's Glorious Guinea*
Owner: Mrs. John Schiff
Breeder: Mrs. P. A. Seager, England
Blenheim Dog

1967 *Pargeter Tessa of Kilspindie*
Owner: Elizabeth Spalding
Breeder: Mrs. B. Keswick, England
Tricolor Bitch

1968 *Olderhill Easter Bon Bon*
Owners: Mr. P. A. Tournaye and
Mr. John Anderson
Breeder: Mrs. A. Butler, England
Blenheim Bitch

1969 *Kilspindie Cheer Up*
Owner/Breeder: Elizabeth Spalding
Blenheim Bitch

1970 *Can. Ch. Pargeter Fergus of Kilspindie*
Owner: Elizabeth Spalding
Breeder: Mrs. B. Keswick, England
Blenheim Dog

1971 *Sartorius Sebastian*
Owners/Breeders: Mr. P. A. Tournaye
and Mr. John Anderson, USA
Blenheim Dog

1972 *Cobblehill Capers*
Owners: Dr. and Mrs. Roma King
Breeder: Miss J. Douglas, England
Tricolor Bitch

1973 *Kilspindie Chalumeau*
Owner/Breeder: Elizabeth Spalding
Blenheim Dog

1974 *Can. Ch. Kilspindie Chalumeau*
Owner/Breeder: Elizabeth Spalding
Blenheim Dog

1975 *Homerbrent Mickey Finn*
Owners: Alice Stenning and
Mary Rose Jepsky
Breeder: Molly Coaker, England
Blenheim Dog

1976   *Can. Ch. Wilblea Cristy*
        Owner: Evelyn R. Bleaney
        Breeders: Evelyn R. Bleaney and
        Mrs. N. Wilson, Canada
        Tricolor Bitch

1977   *Can. Ch. Barings Napoleon of Italia*
        Owner: Mr. W. E. St. Clair
        Breeder: Mrs. M. Patten, England
        Tricolor Dog

1978   *Can. Ch. Dijers Chandlers Snow Knight*
        Owners: Dr. and Mrs. J. Roseff
        Breeder: Mrs. G. Preece, England
        Blenheim Dog

1979   *Chanctonbury Pilgrim*
        Owner: David K. Sterling
        Breeder: Janet Bates, USA
        Blenheim Dog

1980   *Ch. and Can. Ch. Pharos of
        Chandlers & Italia*
        Owner: Janice M. Koehler
        Breeder: Katie Strelcs, England
        Black & Tan Dog

1981   *Can. Ch. Peatland Dasher*
        Owner: Angela Thomas
        Breeder: Mary Millican, England
        Blenheim Dog

1982   *Sanubray Secret Rendezvous of
        Charlescote*
        Owner: Janice M. Koehler
        Breeder: Barbara Spencer, England
        Blenheim Bitch

1983   *Can. Ch. Rocky Raccoon of Wyndcrest*
        Owners: Harold and Joan Letterly
        Breeders: O. Darbyshire and D. Hendrikx,
        Canada
        Blenheim Dog

1984—1986
        *Ch. and Can.Ch. Kindrum Byron
        of Tarryon*
        Owners: Mrs. D. H. Burnham
        and Mr. D. Rubin
        Breeder: Mrs. P. E. Thornhill, England
        Blenheim Dog

1987   *Ch. and Can. Ch. Amantra Naval Salute*
        Owner: Christine Gingell
        Breeder: Mrs. D. Fry, England
        Blenheim Dog

1988   *Ravenrush Darktown Strutter*
        Owners/Breeders: John D. Gammon
        and Robert A. Schroll, USA
        Black & Tan Bitch

*CKCSC, USA/Canadian/Mexican/Americas
and World Champion Rocky Raccoon of
Wyndcrest. Shown at 2 years old after
winning the 1983 CKCSC, USA National
Specialty. Owned by Harold and Joan
Letterly. Photo by Letterly.*

CKCSC, USA and AKC Champion Sheeba Special Edition, 1997 CKCSC, USA National Specialty winner, owned by Karin Ostmann and Ted Eubank. Photo by Gay Glazbrook.

1996   *Dalvreck Dorocha At Flying Colors*
Owner: Cathy J. Gish
Breeder: Mrs. E. McInally, England
Black & Tan Dog

1997   *Ch. Sheeba Special Edition*
Owners: Karin Ostmann and
Ted Eubank
Breeder: Karin Ostmann, USA
Tricolor Dog

*Dogs listed with the championship titles they possessed at the time of winning National. CKCSC, USA titles not instituted until 1977

National Specialty Winners, American Cavalier King Charles Spaniel Club, 1997

1989   *Ch. and Can. Ch. Roydwood Royal Mail*
Owners: Olivia Darbyshire and
Louise Pearce
Breeder: Michael J. Boothroyd, England
Blenheim Dog

1990   *Ravenrush Tartan*
Owners/Breeders: John D. Gammon
and Robert A. Schroll, USA
Blenheim Dog

1991   *Ch. B.J. Holy Terror*
Owner/Breeder: Jo Ann Carvill, USA
Blenheim Dog

1992   *Can. Ch. Laughing Charisma*
Owner/Breeder: Barbara Garnett-
Smith, USA
Blenheim Dog

1993   *Ch. B.J. Holy Terror*
Owner/Breeder: Jo Ann Carvill, USA
Blenheim Dog

1994   *Fair Oaks Fairfield Poseidon*
Owner: Charles H. Minter
Breeder: Christine Meager, USA
Blenheim Dog

1995   *Ch. Rutherford Vivian*
Owner/Breeder: Roberta Jones, USA
Blenheim Bitch

1997   *AKC Ch. Ravenrush Impresario*
Owner: Cynthia Madden
Breeders: John D. Gammon and
Robert A. Schroll, USA
Blenheim Dog

AKC Champion Ravenrush Impresario, 1997 ACKCSC National Specialty winner, owned by Cynthia Madden. Photo by Aries.

Canadian Breed History

The first Cavalier imported to Canada was Deanhill Panda in 1956. The first Cavalier to be shown in the Canadian breed ring after Cavaliers were granted recognition by the Canadian Kennel Club (CKC) in 1957, Panda was bred by Lady Ivor Spencer-Churchill and sent from England to her brother, Mr. C. Cunningham. In 1959, the Cunninghams imported a tricolor bitch from Lady Ivor named Deanhill Gwenevar and mated her with Panda. Thus the first Canadian-bred litter was born. By 1964, the breed was being shown from coast to coast.

Ch. Pargeter Flashback, an English import owned by Sheila Anderson of Victoria, British Columbia, became the first Canadian Champion Cavalier in 1965. In 1970, Can. and Ber. Ch. Newforest Rufus, bred and handled by Mrs. Poppy Steel, became the first Cavalier to attain a Canadian All-Breed Best in Show.

The Cavalier King Charles Spaniel Club of Canada (CKCSCC) was founded in 1973, with founding member Henry Benedetti serving as president. The first National Specialty was held in 1976 in Barrie, Ontario, won by Can. Ch. Kirshaws Dijers Aristides of Janandee, and since that time, specialties have been held in many other provinces, including Quebec, Manitoba, and British Columbia.

In 1980, the CKCSCC awarded its first Breeder of the Decade Award, the criteria for which includes contributions to the advancement of the club as well as achievements in showing, breeding, and obedience. The Wilblea Kennel of Nancy Wilson and Ev Bleaney were the recipients for the 1970s, while Chuck and Carol Purser of Beaverdams Cavaliers won the award for the 1980s. The growth of the CKCSCC is in part a tribute to the efforts of these four members.

National Specialty Winners, Cavalier King Charles Spaniel Club of Canada, 1976 — 1997

1976   *Can. Ch. Kirshaws Dijers Aristides of Janandee*
Owners: Dr. and Mrs. Jerry Roseff
Breeder: Mrs. Kirshaw
Blenheim Dog

1977   *Dijers Chandlers Snow Knight*
Owners: Dr. and Mrs. Jerry Roseff
Breeder: Vera Preece, England
Blenheim Dog

1978   *Can. Ch. Wilblea Brandon*
Owners/Breeders: Evelyn R. Bleaney and Mrs. N. Wilson, Canada
Blenheim Dog

1979   *Can. Ch. Kindrum Solomon Grundy*
Owner: Dr. Clara Tucker
Breeder: Mrs. P. Thornhill, England
Blenheim Dog

1980   *Can. Ch. Stennings Son of Tiger Mountain*
Owners/Breeders: Alice Stenning Warden and Mary Rose Stenning Jepsky, Canada
Blenheim Dog

1981   *Can. Ch. Beaverdams Edward*
Owners/Breeders: Chuck and Carol Purser, Canada
Blenheim Dog

Canadian and CKCSC, USA Champion B.J. Garbo.
1984 Canadian National Specialty winner,
owned by Ev Bleaney. Photo by Carvill.

1982   *Can. Ch. Peatland Dasher*
        Owner: Angela Thomas
        Breeder: Mary Millican, England
        Blenheim Dog

1983   *Ch. and Can. Ch. Brookdale Shamrock*
        of Beaverdam
        Owners: Chuck and Carol Purser
        Breeder: Lesley Gogarty, USA
        Blenheim Dog

1984   *Ch. and Can. Ch. B.J. Garbo*
        Owner: Evelyn Bleaney
        Breeder: Jo Ann Carvill, USA
        Blenheim Bitch

CKCSC, USA and Canadian Champion Kindrum Sylvester at Brynwood, 1994 Canadian National Specialty winner, owner Courtney Carter. Photo by Alex Smith Photography.

1985   *Can. Ch. Beaverdam Love Song*
        Owners/Breeders: Chuck and Carol
        Purser
        Blenheim Dog

1986   *Can. Ch. Glenrobin Hamish of Kewpy*
        Owner: Karen Wills
        Breeders: Evelyn Bleaney, Canada
        Blenheim Dog

1987   *Can. Ch. Beaverdam Fanfare*
        Owners/Breeders: Chuck and Carol
        Purser, Canada
        Blenheim Dog

1988   *Can. Ch. Ricksbruy Cool Operator*
        Owner: Angela Thomas
        Breeders: Messers. Rix and Berry, Eng.
        Blenheim Dog

1989   *Ch. and Can. Ch. Roydwood Royal Mail*
        Owners: Olivia Darbyshire and
        Louise Pearce
        Breeder: Michael J. Boothroyd, England
        Blenheim Dog

1990   *Can. Ch. Mostyn Spencer for Hire*
        Owner: Phyllis Short
        Breeder: Brigida Reynolds, Canada
        Tricolor Dog

1991   *Can. Ch. Amantra Disco to Go*
        Owners: Olivia Darbyshire and
        Louise Pearce
        Breeder: Mrs. D. Fry, England
        Tricolor Dog

1992   *Can. Ch. Cinola Blondie*
        Owner: Dorcas Mycock
        Breeder: Barbara Evans, England
        Blenheim Bitch

1993   *Can. Ch. Muffity Ollie at Brynwood*
        Owner: Courtney Carter
        Breeder: Jenny Hall, England
        Blenheim Dog

1994   *Ch. and Can. Ch. Kindrum Sylvester*
        at Brynwood
        Owner: Courtney Carter
        Breeder: Mrs. P. E. Thornhill, England
        Blenheim Dog

1995   *Can. Ch. Kewpy's ZZ Top*
        of Cambridge
        Owners: Karen Wills and Elaine Mitchell
        Breeder: Karen Wills, Canada
        Blenheim Dog

1996   *Can. Ch. Glenorchy's Titannias Gold*
        Owner/Breeder Ann Chambers, Canada
        Blenheim Bitch

1997   *Can. Ch. Madrigal It's Magic*
        Owner/Breeder: Beverly Dent,
        Canada
        Blenheim Dog

Influential English Kennels

Over the years, some of England's top kennels have sent some outstanding Cavaliers to Canada and the United States. From these dogs and the dedication of their owners, the North American Cavalier King Charles Spaniel has risen to a level of excellence that is competitive with Cavaliers all over the world. Mrs. Keswick's Pargeters were of unrivaled importance in the early Cavaliers in Canada and the United States, but in the last twenty years, the greatest influence has been from the kennels listed here, in alphabetical order.

The Amantras

Bred by the mother daughter team of Di Fry and Tracy Jackson, the Amantras have been influential on North American Cavaliers. Mrs. Olivia Darbyshire's Canadian Ch. Amantra Pinball Wizard sired Joan and Harold Letterly's great Canadian, Mexican, Bermuda, CKCSC, USA and World Ch. Rocky Raccoon of Wyndcrest, one of the best known Cavaliers in the history of the breed in both Canada and the US. Many of the Amantras imported became champions, and have produced champions themselves. Gentle heads with soft expressions, correct size and superb temperaments were the strengths of this kennel. Some imports included Chuck Minter's Amantra Coastguard of Fairfield, Anne and Jane Thaeder's English and Australian Ch. Amantra Captain Pugwash, Chris Gingell's Canadian and CKCSC, USA Ch. Amantra Naval Salute, Barbara Garnett-

Smith's Canadian and CKCSC, USA Ch. Amantra Some Dame of Laughing and Canadian and CKCSC, USA Ch. Amantra Sweet Fantasy of Laughing.

CKCSC, USA and Canadian Champion Amantra Sweet Fantasy of Laughing. Owned by the author. Photo by Vavra.

Canadian Champion Amantra Coastguard at Fairfield. Owned by Charles Minter. Photo by Fall.

The Crisdigs

It is would be difficult to sufficiently stress the importance of Brigadier and Mrs. Jack Burgess' Crisdigs on Cavaliers worldwide. Only a few Crisdigs actually came to North America, but those who did certainly made their mark. Miss Elizabeth Spalding's Kilspindie Cavaliers were based on a combination of Crisdig and Pargeter lines, producing some outstanding Cavaliers, such as Canadian and CKCSC, USA Ch. Kilspindie Mockingbird. Mr. and Mrs. David Burnham's Crisdig McButtons daughter, Kilspindie Charmaine of Tarryon, was the first CKCSC, USA champion. Many of the top North American Cavaliers go back directly to the Crisdig line, and in fact, an enormous percentage of the CKCSC, USA champions to date have some Crisdig blood behind them.

Crisdig Tony of Hurleaze and Saintbrides. Owned by Pam Burkley. Photo by Burkley.

The Haranas

One cannot say wholecolor in North America without saying Harana. From the beginning, Diana and Lucy Koster said they would never export any dog that they would not want to keep themselves, and having kept their word, the Haranas have brought wholecolors international attention. They have sent some outstanding Cavaliers particularly to the USA, some of which are Denise Quittmeyers Canadian and CKCSC, USA Ch. Harana Freddie Starr; Kathy Gentil's Ruby, Harana Courtney; Courtney Carter's Black and Tan CKCSC, USA Ch. Harana Charlie Parker at Brynwood; CKCSC, USA and Canadian Ch. Harana Horace at Brynwood and CKCSC, USA and Canadian Ch. Harana Jeremy Dortmund at Brynwood.

CKCSC, USA and Canadian Champion Harana Freddie Starr. Owned by Denise Quittmeyer. Photo by Digital Artistry.

The Homarannes and Homerbrents

Another mother daughter team, Molly Coaker (Homerbrent) and Anne Reddaway (Homaranne) have produced some legendary Cavaliers. Type, glorious heads, health, glamour and longevity are the legacy of these two kennels. While few have actually been exported to Canada and the USA, their influence cannot be denied, as so many of the top Cavaliers on both sides of the Atlantic have Homerbrent or Homaranne breeding behind them.

English Champion Homerbrent Festival. Owned by Mrs. Molly Coaker, England. Photo by Coaker.

English Champion Homaranne Caption. Owned by Mrs. Molly Coaker, England. Photo by Coaker.

The Kindrums

There is hardly a kennel of importance in North America that has not been influenced in one manner or another by Pam Thornhill's Kindrum Cavaliers. The Kindrums are known for exceptional type and glamour, but their greatest gift has been their incredible eyes, which are apparent in generations of North American Cavaliers with Kindrum blood behind them. Some of the best known imports from the Kindrum Kennel have been the Burnham's Canadian and CKCSC, USA Ch. Kindrum Byron of Tarryon, Miriam Lovet's Canadian and CKCSC, USA Ch. Kindrum Archie Tec of Primrose, Robbi Jones Canadian and CKCSC, USA Ch. Kindrum Lucifer of Rutherford, Courtney Carter's Canadian and CKCSC, USA Champion Kindrum Sylvester at Brynwood, the Schiffman's Canadian and CKCSC, USA Champion Kindrum Marcus of Crossbow, and the influential brood bitches, Canadian Champion Kindrum Alice of Rutherford and Kindrum Savannah of Crossbow, owned by Robbi Jones and David and Wesely Schiffman respectively.

English Champion Alberto of Kindrum. Owned by Mrs. Pam Thornhill, England. Photo by Thornhill.

The Maxholts

Mrs. Peggy Talbot's Maxholt Cavaliers were known for their distinctive heads, overall type and longevity. Some of the outstanding Maxholts that were imported to the USA were Pat Winters CKCSC, USA Ch. Maxholt Silver Secret of Cobblestone and Canadian and CKCSC, USA Ch. Snuff Box of Maxholt and Cobblestone, CD; Janet York's CKCSC, USA, Canadian, BDA, SKC, CDA Ch. Maxholt Special Love Story, UDX; and C. Anne Robins bitch, Canadian and CKCSC, USA Ch. Maxholt Special Secret of Chadwick.

Mrs. Peggy Talbot with her Maxholts.
Photo by John Talbot.

The Saladors

Known for their type, soundness and elegance, the Saladors have had a profound influence on the breed in both Canada and the USA. While only a few Saladors have been imported to North America, those few have left an indelible legacy, apparent in dogs such as Gammon and Schroll's CKCSC, USA Champion Ravenrush Tartan, Cindy Lazzeroni's CKCSC, USA and AKC Ch. Partridge Wood Laughing Misdemeanour, Martha Guimond's Canadian and CKCSC, USA Ch. Rutherford Elliot of Shagbark, and Barbara Garnett-Smith's Canadian and CKCSC, USA Champion Laughing Charisma.

English Champion Salador Celtic Prince.
Owned by Sheila Smith, England. Photo by Pearce.

English Champion Salador Crismark.
Owned by Sheila Smith, England. Photo by Dalton.

A Champion Arabian mare and her canine companions owned by Mike Lamb.
True to his sporting nature, the Cavalier enjoys an outing on the trail. Photo by Jay Gross Photography.

chapter two

LIVING WITH A CAVALIER

Cavaliers are gifted with a playful, gentle, endearing nature. They possess a remarkable ability to adapt to almost any situation, making them suitable for country or city living. They are happy as long as they are close to their master, by whose side they are always content. Cavaliers love to go for hikes, to swim, to run, and to play ball, but once they are back in the comfort of home, they are

Laughing Lord Woodstock, exemplifying the breed's joyful disposition. Owned by Rebecca Field. Photo by Rebecca Field.

generally calm, spending hours asleep in a favorite spot on the family couch or armchair.

We have seen our Cavaliers grow from puppy to adult to old age in the years we have lived in the mountains of Oregon, and we have been amazed at how incredibly athletic and generally

healthy the breed is. Given the advantage of almost unlimited space to run and play, our Cavaliers have had every opportunity to develop healthy lungs, hearts, and bodies, yet they have had the same opportunity to develop the problems caused by physical or structural weaknesses. They have not all gone through life trouble free, but generally speaking, they have rarely had to go to the vet and are seldom anything other than in fine condition. It is important to realize that while so much is written about health problems in purebred dogs, Cavaliers are as healthy, and probably more so, as many other breeds today.

Cavaliers with Other Pets and Children

The small, sturdy size and gentle, playful personality of the Cavalier makes this breed an excellent choice for a family with children. When a Cavalier is confronted by one or more children, the safety of the children is not the concern as much as the safety of the Cavalier! A Cavalier is ready to submit to the roughest treatment without fighting back or even running away due to his sweetness and lack of aggression. A good breeder will take particular care in choosing a puppy for a young family.

Cavaliers do especially well in pairs, being wonderful company for each other. If you already own another dog with a friendly temperament, you will be amazed by the relationship that the two will form. When a second dog is introduced into a household, the first dog may sulk for as long as two or three weeks, but eventually they will play

Cavaliers are an excellent choice for a family with children. Emily Garnett with her puppy, Daisy. Photo by the author.

together by the hour and often end up sharing the same bed.

Cavaliers and cats can be surprisingly good companions. When first introduced, the Cavalier will approach the cat, at which time the cat will put out its claws and with hair on end, hiss threateningly. The Cavalier will quickly understand this message and take his distance. The cat will maintain his new companion under constant observation, usually from the top of a piece of furniture, but eventually the first step toward friendly relations will be taken. All of this will end in games and snores from the same basket.

Housing

Cavaliers have been bred for centuries to be companions, making them ideal house pets and family members. They do not thrive in kennels or being shut away from those whom they love. A securely fenced area is essential, as without a thought of danger, a Cavalier will run straight in front of a moving car to see a person on the other side of the road.

Exercise Requirements

Cavaliers thrive on exercise. While they love to sit by the fire, they should be given the opportunity to run and play freely in the fresh air every day in order to maintain their best physical and mental condition. If space does not allow this,

and weather permits, they should be taken for a good walk. No Cavalier should ever live it's life in a crate, kennel or tied on a stake.

Caution does need to be taken when encountering strange dogs while out of the home environment, because Cavaliers have what can be an unnerving lack of fear or respect for other dogs, regardless of size.

Grooming

Cavaliers require surprisingly little grooming compared with similarly coated breeds, but they should be given at least one thorough brushing every week. They don't need a bath more than once a month, although this can depend on what they get into. Several of mine just came in from a frolic in the pasture and are lying at my feet, radiating a heavy aroma of horse manure. Not much doubt as to where they will be before the end of the day, regardless of the date of their last bath!

Dimples to Sparky...."Just act natural, no one will ever notice!" Some clean-ups make take a little longer than others. Whether it is warm and sunny or cold and snowy, our Laughing Cavaliers enjoy life to the fullest. Photo by the author.

Cavaliers are a natural breed and require no clipping or trimming. They shed a moderate amount, but at worst, their shedding can be kept to a bearable amount with minimal grooming. Often referred to as "wash-and-wear" dogs, Cavaliers will clean up quickly even from their muddiest outdoor adventures when they are given a bath.

Traveling

Cavaliers make excellent traveling companions. They are the ideal size for motor homes and are usually small enough to fly underneath the seat on an airplane. They seldom, if ever, need to be tranquilized. For underseat airline travel, a large sized soft-sided carrier is the most suitable for an adult Cavalier. These are available through catalogs and at pet stores.

Cavaliers make excellent traveling companions. CKCSC, USA Ch. Chadwick Great Balls of Fire, owned by Denise and Richard Quittmeyer. Photo by Anne Robins.

Cavaliers love to ride in cars but do not tolerate extreme heat, therefore they must never be left in an unattended car in hot weather, due to the risk of heat prostration. Dognapping is also becoming an increasing danger for unattended pets.

Barking

Cavaliers greet everyone with the same enthusiastic welcome, so they should not be expected to fulfill the duties of a watchdog. They are not yappy and seldom bark without reason, but they will give warning when a stranger is approaching. I heard of someone who lived with this breed in the fifteenth story of an apartment in a big city. It was only when she acquired her seventh Cavalier that she decided to move to a house in the country! Her dogs were never the slightest problem, and her neighbors swore that

they would never have been aware that she had seven Cavaliers had she not needed to ride the elevator to take them for their walks.

Only one time were all of ours struck dumb. When I was first married, I thought that I wanted a mountain lion cub as a pet, but my husband wouldn't even consider the idea. One day years later, Bob came home grinning hugely, saying that he had arranged for me to have what I always wanted. I was filled with curiosity, but before my imagination had run to sports cars and the like, down the driveway came a huge pickup truck, the whole back taken up by a cage containing an enormous cat—the mountain lion cub I had dreamed about, full grown. Every one of our Cavaliers lined up on the driveway fence, and not one of them uttered so much as a squeak. They sat in frozen horror as the enormous cat licked its lips in glorious anticipation of tricolor for breakfast, Blenheim for lunch, ruby for afternoon tea, and black and tan for dinner. The owner assured me that the cat was oh! so tame with children (except perhaps at meal time), and gentle, sweet, and kind in all ways (except perhaps at mealtime). For once, common sense reigned and the dream-come-true was sent back down the driveway, with all of the Cavaliers, brave once more, giving howling chase.

The Versatile Cavalier
Cavaliers in the Field

All Breed Standards for the Cavalier King Charles Spaniel include the words "sporting in character," and while the greatest emphasis is placed on Cavaliers as companion dogs, their least-known attribute is a natural hunting instinct. They could not spend several centuries in English drawing rooms without losing a bit of hunting instinct, but this has not been totally eradicated. Cavaliers are relatively easy to train, they are not gun-shy, they have good mouths, and are reportedly quite clever at finding and flushing game birds.

The red-and-white Blenheim Spaniel, a dog with an excellent reputation for flushing out

The hunting instinct of the Cavalier has not been eradicated. Metcroft Tyler, owned by Rosemary Dunstall, retrieves a pheasant. Photo by Dunstall.

gatherer—perhaps the reason why some of the sporting spaniels have docked tails. Several of our Cavaliers are used by their owners for flushing quail and chukker and apparently are successful at retrieving small game. We know from experience that Cavaliers love to get wet and dirty, so they are in their element on a chilly damp morning with plenty of puddles and the enticement of a bird or rabbit ahead. While actively searching for game, Cavaliers will often adopt the traditional hunting pose of pointing. Ears high, tail up, eyes glinting with anticipation, they are a sight to behold. Currently, a group is forming with the hope of seeing Cavaliers in field competition. Perhaps, as it was pointed out so long ago, "there they ought oftener to be."

Cavaliers as Therapy Dogs

The value of pets to the psychological health of human beings is becoming increasingly well known. Practitioners who make use of this benign influence refer to animal-assisted therapy, which is used in a number of health-care environments, including hospitals, nursing homes, homes for the elderly, and institutions for the handicapped. The gentle disposition of the Cavalier, combined with the most salient characteristic of the breed—its lovableness—makes this dog the ideal therapeutic companion. Canada's Mary Konkle, along with numerous other good-hearted Canadian and American Cavalier owners, has brought joy and happiness to many less fortunate people by visiting hospitals and nursing homes with their Cavaliers.

Titles can be earned such as Canine Good Citizen (CGC), Temperament Test (TT), and registered Therapy Dog (TDI), some of which are required for visiting nursing homes and people in hospitals.

game, was developed for hunting by the first Duke of Marlborough. More than a hundred years ago, Youatt wrote this about them: "From its beauty and occasional gaiety, the Blenheim Spaniel is oftener an inhabitant of the drawing room than the field. But it occasionally breaks out and shows what nature designed it for. Some of these carpeted pets acquit themselves nobly in the covert. There they ought oftener to be."

One enthusiast reports that her Cavalier loves traditional hunting activities such as lure coursing, tracking, flushing, and finding birds in the grass. She also says that the Cavalier's size and full coat are a disadvantage in the field, because a beautifully plumed tail makes a great weed

Canada's Joan Branscombe has worked in the health-care environment for years. Mrs. Branscombe's tricolor Cavalier, Carlo was her invaluable assistant when she worked at a health-care facility in Tofield, Alberta. Wherever she went, Carlo was always willing to greet people with a friendly tail-wag and to sit on their lap if invited. He would faithfully make each nursing round, and if a room was missed, he would sit at the door and wait until someone returned to check the resident asleep in that room.

Carlo was at Mrs. Branscombe's side when they entered the room of a lady who was being admitted to the hospital with advanced Alzheimer's disease. The stress and tension were palpable. The new resident was sitting on the bed, wide-eyed and fearful, not comprehending where she was or why she was there. Her husband and daughter were standing by the bed, obviously not knowing what to say or do, tears streaming down their faces. Carlo, who was never allowed on the resident's bed unless invited, seemed to sense the anxiety and

St. James Champagne of Hummingbird,
"Lili" the therapy dog with Grace P. Darrah.
Owner: Rachel D. Richard.

hopped up on the bed, nestling down beside the frightened little lady. She began stroking his head and back, then suddenly her face broke into a smile and the tension evaporated. Carlo retired in March 1995, having brought pleasure to many lives for more than eight years.

Cavaliers in Canine Freestyle Ballet

Invented in Canada, canine freestyle ballet was introduced to the United States in 1993, where it became an instant success. Freestyle guru and Cavalier owner Joan Tennille defines this new art in the following way:

> "The objective of Freestyle is to showcase the dog to his best advantage in a creative and artistic manner. Freestyle should demonstrate, with appropriate music, the grace, beauty and intelligence of the dog working in harmony with the handler. A Freestyle presentation should clearly show the dog's gaits, athleticism, attentiveness and flexibility. These elements are judged by the freedom and regularity of the movements, well marked and rhythmic. While teamwork is essential, all handler movements should compliment and enhance the dog's movements."

Cavaliers in Agility

Agility as a sporting event, was introduced at England's Crufts dog show in 1978. Inspired by equestrian gymkhana events, agility was initially used to amuse the spectators while they were awaiting the judging of Best in Show. John Varley designed an obstacle course, and it was so successful that the tradition has continued as an event in itself. Cavalier owners take enormous pleasure in agility, which the Cavalier takes as a game.

A large variety of obstacles can be included in an agility trial, such as balance beams, tunnels, jumps, and A-frames that have to be scaled. To bound through the center of a tire or fly over jumps, to slalom between posts or run through a tunnel—none of these maneuvers will phase the Cavalier in the slightest.

There are three levels of competition—novice, open and excellent. The number and complexity of obstacles increase with each level, as does the speed required to run the course, because it must be run in the shortest time possible. Agility can help build a dog's confidence and is wonderful for those who have become bored with competitive obedience. It increases offleash control of a dog and is excellent exercise for both dog and owner. Because most Cavaliers are so mentally stable, they make ideal candidates for the sport and as long as they are kept in excellent condition—can continue to compete for years.

Cavaliers in Obedience

The willingness of Cavaliers to please makes them good candidates for obedience competition. Benefits of obedience training are better manners and control, but above all, obedience enhances the relationship between dog and handler. The training for competitive obedience can be very time consuming and requires the utmost patience of the handler and requires a dog that is both intelligent and athletic—both traits that are indicative of the Cavalier.

The beginning level of obedience competition is Novice. The dog is required to complete individual exercises while on and off the lead. They are judged on their ability to stay with their handler in "heel" position, stand still for a hands-on examination by the judge and to come when called by the handler.

The second level of competition is Open. All exercises are done off lead, including heeling, dropping on recall, retrieving a dumbbell on the flat and over a high jump, jumping a broad jump and participating in group sits and downs while the handlers are out of sight.

The highest level in obedience competition is Utility. Dogs are required to complete complex patterns while off lead combining heeling and hand signal exercises. Dogs must be able to scent retrieve articles recently touched by their handler, do a directed retrieve, correctly picking up one of three gloves, and conclude with jumping a high-bar and high-jump as directed through hand-signals from their handler.

A perfect score in all obedience competitions is 200—points are subtracted for dogs that stray from heel position, sits that are not straight, sits that are too slow or that don't happen at all, dogs that move from a position before being released by their handler, and in the higher levels of competition, points will be deducted for hitting jumps, playing with the dumbbell, and cutting corners on jumps. Handlers can also incur penalty points from the initial score of 200. A dog must achieve a score of 170 points or better, to be awarded a qualifying score, often called a "leg." A dog and handler must earn 3 such legs, under three different judges, to earn the title of CD or Companion Dog for novice competition, CDX or Companion Dog Excellent for open competition and UD or Utility Dog for utility competition. Dogs with their UD title may continue to compete in both open and utility classes, collecting points to achieve the title of OTCh or Obedience Trial Champion.

Cavaliers first began competing in the AKC in 1962. The first American Cavalier to achieve a UD and TD (Tracking Dog title) was Shaggy Mead's Lord Chancellor, owned and trained by Katharin Foster of Athens, Ohio. He earned his TD in 1977. Felicity of Boxford, CDX, TDX, TT-l, the first Cavalier to achieve a Tracking Dog Excellent title, was also owned and trained by the Fosters. In 1994, the title of Utility Dog Excellent was offered by the AKC, and U-UD Saintbrides Trifle, UDX, CGC, TT, owned by Terri and Sandi Atkinson, became the first Cavalier to accomplish this amazing feat. In 1996, the CKCSC, USA implemented its own Obedience Award system.

The first Canadian Cavalier to achieve a UD and TT was Ch. Picbrand Mardi Gras, OTCh, TT, owned and trained by Paul Oslach and bred by Don and Shirley Kitchen.

*Janet York and Ch. Maxholt Special Love Story, UDX
AKA "Piccadilly" perform Canine Freestyle Ballet.
Photo by York.*

*St. James Champagne of Hummingbird, "Lili" the agility dog.
Proudly owned by Rachel Richard. Photo by Kathy Pepin.*

*Ch. Maxholt Special Love Story, UDX.
Owned by Janet York. Photo by York.*

President and Mrs. Ronald Reagan with their Cavalier "Rex."
Photo courtesy President and Mrs. Ronald Reagan.

chapter three

CHOOSING THE RIGHT CAVALIER

*B*efore adopting a Cavalier puppy, discuss your family's willingness to accept the responsibilities of dog ownership. Having a puppy join the family is not dissimilar to bringing a new baby into the house, and it requires some commitment on the part of everyone. Children may make promises about feeding and walking a dog, but inevitably this task will fall to the adults. Allergies or an aversion to dog hair need to be

considered, as well as the fact that Cavaliers must have a securely fenced yard. Although someone does not need to be home at all times, arrangements will have to be made for a puppy to be exercised and fed if he is left alone for more than a few hours. While a conscientious breeder will maintain an interest in each puppy throughout it's lifetime and will offer to re-home the puppy should an emergency arise, it must be clearly understood that adopting a puppy is a lifetime commitment. Dogs are not disposable commodities.

Once you decide to acquire a Cavalier, your first step is to locate a reputable breeder.

Choosing a Breeder

Choosing a breeder is one of the most important decisions you will make when adopting a Cavalier puppy, so choose carefully. Never be tempted to buy a Cavalier from a pet store, as the sort of breeder that you want to have bred and raised your puppy would never place a Cavalier in a situation where, at the very least, they had no idea where their puppy was going, or to whom. Don't buy one out of pity for the poor little puppy in the window, because if you do, another one will take its place immediately! To buy a puppy in a pet store encourages the mass producing of puppies by unscrupulous puppy millers, and encourages commercial breeding by back-yard-breeders who give no thought to anything other than the bottom line.

Reputable breeders are willing to answer any questions about Cavaliers in general and about

Shamrock kissing Shannon. When a family includes children it is important that consideration is given to sturdiness and an appropriate disposition. Photo by Monica Cantwell.

Litter of six week old Blenheim puppies. Photo by Barb Hoorman

their own dogs specifically. In turn, you must be prepared to answer questions about yourself and your family, as the fundamental goal of a caring breeder is the welfare of his puppies. It may not always be possible to physically visit breeders who have been recommended, but whether or not the breeder is in the same town or across the country, it is very important that a good rapport exist between you.

It is amazing how many calls we get from people who do not even know the proper name of the Cavalier. Although sometimes the word combinations that come up are amusing, it is often hard to take someone seriously who calls inquiring about a "King Cavalier," a "Cavalier St. Charles," a "St. Charles Cooker" or worse, "You know, the dog that is a cross between a Cocker Spaniel and a Pekinese!"

Choosing a Cavalier as a Companion

Choosing a puppy whose primary purpose is to be a companion is quite different from choosing one that is eventually going into the show ring. Lifestyle, city or country, apartment or house, play an important role in establishing the criteria for the ideal companion. Some people want a puppy that is quiet and gentle, while others want a merry, fun-loving one that laughs its way through life. There can also be strong feelings about male or female and about specific physical characteristics such as color and size. When a family includes children, it is important that

Hilary, Whitney and Cameron Gee with their Cavalier companions. Photo by Vavra.

Stormy and Cassie sharing Colin's bath. Owned by Dr. and Mrs. Scott Harper. Photo by Harper.

consideration is given to the sturdiness and an appropriate disposition of the puppy.

Sometimes people will come to see the puppies and ask that the entire litter be brought out so that they can choose the puppy that they want. It is better to place your confidence in the chosen breeder, who knows the strengths and weaknesses of his puppies. The more you talk to the breeder ahead of time, the more you will reveal your likes and dislikes. Let the breeder select the right puppy for you.

Many of the points that determine whether a Cavalier is suitable for showing are usually of such a technical nature as to be unnoticeable and most often unimportant to the average pet owner. My parents were a perfect example of this. Their Cavalier was a very pretty little dog, although he was not a show dog. It never made any difference how many ribbons or trophies we came home with, my father would always look at the dog that had just won, then would look at his own Cavalier and say, " I simply don't understand it. He is not nearly as pretty as my Ted!"

Male or Female

Male and female Cavaliers make equally good pets. The saying "females love you, males are in love with you" has some truth in it, but one does not make a better pet than the other. When making the decision between male and female, unless there is an aversion to a particular sex, the specific disposition of a puppy should be the determining factor.

Spaying and neutering are recommended when a Cavalier is being placed as a companion and is not going to be shown and bred, because it makes for a happy, healthier pet. A female should be spayed before her first heat season, six months being the recommended age. Spaying before the first season decreases the risk of mammary cancer as well as eliminates the nuisance of the season itself. Males should be neutered no later than six months of age to reduce the risk of testicular and prostate cancer and also to avert territorial male behavior. Males that are not neutered young may

Spayed due to a medical emergency, a champion bitch was able to continue her show career as a result of the CKCSC, USA rule allowing spayed and neutered Cavaliers to compete in conformation competition. Shown winning Reserve Best in Show in March 1997, CKCSC, USA Ch. Laughing Society Dame at Benchmark. Owned by Barb Hoorman. Photo by Digital Artistry.

still be interested in in-season bitches and will occasionally even mount them.

More and more veterinarians in the United States and Canada are opting for early spaying and neutering––some as early as eight weeks. Spaying and neutering should not make a Cavalier fat or lazy, although the amount of food offered should be decreased due to a lower metabolism. Spaying and neutering will generally cause an increase in coat volume and a change of coat texture.

To encourage spaying and neutering, the CKCSC, USA (but not the AKC or CKC) allows spayed and neutered Cavaliers to be shown in conformation classes at Championship shows, a rule which has been in place in England for some time.

Picking the Show Puppy

Before choosing a potential show puppy, carefully read the Breed Standard and become familiar with the ideal breed characteristics of the Cavalier. The best way to accomplish this is to attend as many shows as possible. When you are choosing a puppy that will hopefully grow into a show stopper, there are certain qualities that must be present from the beginning: basic conformation,

Promising seven week old Tricolor puppies. Photo by the author.

The ear leathers on all Cavalier puppies should be long and full. Photo by Eubank.

Eight week old Ruby puppies. Photo by the author.

combined with that most important attitude and charisma.

It is important to find a breeder with whom you have a level of comfort and trust—a breeder who is willing to act as a mentor before, during, and after you choose your puppy. While it is virtually impossible for even the most seasoned breeder to say categorically that an eight- to twelve-week-old puppy is going to grow up to be a show dog, the eye that is trained from experience will almost always recognize star quality.

Personality

A dog that is going to show must have an exuberant disposition, which will be apparent from quite a young age. Choose a puppy that is full of confidence.

Color

Don't be fooled into thinking that a puppy has show potential just because he is well marked and has a Blenheim spot. Refer to the Standard for requirements of each color. Our Alansmere Rhett Butler, an English, Canadian, and CKCSC, USA champion had a good-sized smudge on the side of

his muzzle. Yet, who could overlook such a wonderful dog due to a small cosmetic irregularity?

The ear leathers of Blenheim puppies are more indicative of the adult coat color than is their body color. When born, some can be almost pale lemon colored, but this darkens with age. Those that are going to be a rich, deep red are that way from birth. The red color should be broken up (well spaced) with white, and the markings on the head should ideally be even. A Blenheim spot or lozenge is considered the icing on the cake but is not required. Ticking on both Blenheims and tricolors frequently may not be apparent when puppies are less than four months old. The "pearly white" of Blenheims and tricolors described in the Standard is exactly that—not a blue white, but the warm white of a well-colored pearl.

The black of tricolors tends to invade the white as the puppies mature, so if the blaze between the eyes is not fairly wide from the start, it will often close completely by adulthood. The black on the body also needs to be interspersed with a good amount of white. Tan markings, which should be rich and bright, must be over the eyes, on the cheeks, inside the ears, and on the underside of the tail.

The great show dogs will have a "look" and a presence that cannot be denied. English, Canadian and CKCSC, USA Champion Alansmere Rhett Butler. Owned by the author. Photo by Gordon Inglis.

An example of a well marked tricolor, Canadian and AKC Champion Grantilley Dollar, owned by Lou Samuels. Photo by David Gossett.

Ruby puppies can be lighter in color on the body, but again, it is the ear leathers that are indicative of what is to come. The richest-colored rubies are that way from birth. Black and tans should be raven black with tan markings above the eyes, on the cheeks, inside the ears, on the chest and legs, and on the underside of the tail, although their tan markings are sometimes paler than they will be as adults. White patches on rubies and black and tans usually lessen drastically from puppy-hood. Small patches usually go away entirely, with the exception of large white patches on the bridge of the nose, under the chin, and on the chest. A ruby or black and tan that is born with white feet will often end up with solid feet, although pads under the foot may be mottled. I would personally prefer to have an excellent specimen with a small amount of white than I would a lesser specimen with no white.

Any other color or combination of colors is unacceptable, particularly a "chocolate" tricolor, in which the black has a reddish tinge and the eyes often have an ugly yellowish hue.

Coat

Coat is genetically determined, both in length and texture. Weather and living conditions can contribute to length and even curliness, but a Cavalier that does not have the genes for a good coat will never attain the same quantity and quality as the individual that was bred for it. The properly textured coat is silky and straight, while the coarser coat will tend to curliness. Young puppies can have "teddy-bear" coats, but this is not particularly significant. It is sometimes said that if a puppy has a heavy amount of hair on its back skull, he will be heavily coated as an adult. True?
Sometimes!

Head Type

An experienced breeder will recognize the desired head type almost from birth. The head of a puppy should have a nice breadth to it, and the nose should be neither too long nor too short. Ear leathers should be long and ideally, when pulled forward, will reach the tip of the nose. Eyes should be round and, properly spaced and should appear large in proportion to the head. Depth of eye color may be difficult to ascertain in a youngster, so the eye color of the parents should be the gauge.

The most frustrating determination to make is the bite. A bite that is correct at eight weeks should be correct when the second teeth come in, but unfortunately, this is not always the case. Family background plays a major role, but luck also enters the equation. Cavalier bites can change until as late as two years of age, so there is plenty of time to hope or worry. The Canadian Breed Standard for the Cavalier allows a level bite, as does that of the CKCSC, USA. The AKC Standard requires a full scissors bite, as does the English one.

Nose pigment should be black, with no tinge of pink or brown. Small white marks on the nose, called "butterfly" noses, will usually disappear by two years of age, although large patches of white never will.

Structure

The body of a Cavalier puppy should not appear long. The front legs should not seem to be set too wide apart, nor should feet toe in, toe out, or be curved in appearance. Elbows should be set tightly into the body. Back legs should be straight when viewed from the rear, with a short hock and no tendency to turn in at the hock in or bow out. When viewed from the side, stifles should not appear straight. Angulation should not be extreme, front or rear.

The head should be carried proudly on a moderately long neck. The Standard calls for moderate bone, which means neither too fine nor too heavy. Large feet in a puppy may indicate a large adult, although the size of the puppies can be misleading (we had one named Tinker Bell who grew to be nearly thirty pounds, and one named Moose who ended up well within the Standard).

Young puppies tend to use their tails for balance, so at seven to eight weeks old, watch the puppy playing freely. If the tail tends to curl up over the back, the tail set will probably be incorrect upon examination. If the tail set is neither too high nor too low and the topline is correct, the tail will not be gay.

Males must have both testicles descended into the scrotum, but this may not occur until four to five months of age.

The Perfect Specimen

There is no such thing as the perfect specimen! Very often the novice fancier (and sometimes a judge) becomes obsessed with faults and will overlook a dog of stellar quality. The great all-breed judge Anne Rogers Clark once said, "All dogs have faults. Great ones wear them well."

Cavalier Rescue

The purpose of Cavalier Rescue is to house all homeless and unwanted Cavalier King Charles Spaniels in foster homes, providing proper medical care and evaluation until a permanent adoptive home can be found. A loving, supportive, nurturing home that will restore the Cavalier to complete physical and mental health is a primary criteria in the search for adopting families.

Cavaliers generally maintain their sweet dispositions and trusting natures in spite of the indignities sometimes suffered at the hands of their human caretakers. This makes them exceptionally well suited to quickly adjust to a new home environment. A rescue organization may therefore be a good place to look for a Cavalier. Cavaliers are usually able to adapt quickly and they offer their unconditional love wholeheartedly. Even those with varying degrees of medical problems are uncomplaining and ask only to be loved.

Any individuals who find that they are unable to continue caring for their Cavalier are urged to call the breeder first and foremost. As a second resort they should contact their club rescue service to ensure that the dog is placed in a loving home, rather than to abandon him to the streets or animal shelters.

If you find a stray Cavalier, or even hear about one, contact Cavalier Rescue immediately. A large part of their service is to reunite lost Cavaliers with their rightful owners.

In Canada, all Cavaliers are required by federal law to be microchipped or tattooed. This practice is also being encouraged in the U.S. Not only does it discourage dogknapping but it also allows the identification and return of lost Cavaliers.

AKC Champion Hometown Ever Hopeful at Millhill, owned by Janet Dalton. Photo by Janet Dalton.

Chadwick Backgammon with Harvey, the Birman kitten, owned by Anne Robins. Photo by Robins.

chapter four

THE NEW CAVALIER PUPPY

*T*here are a few things that you can do ahead of time to help make the arrival of your Cavalier puppy a more enjoyable experience.

Equipment

Before the puppy arrives, you will need a water bowl, food bowl (both preferably stainless steel or glazed crockery), a bed, a supply of food recommended by the breeder, a soft brush or comb, and, of course, toys. Cavalier puppies love plushy lambswool toys with squeakers, rope pulls, and anything they can chew, such as Cheweez, available at grocery stores.

Providing the puppy with a warm, den-like place in which he can feel secure is the best way to acclimate a puppy to his new environment. Buy a kennel or crate for this purpose and have it ready so that the puppy will know that this is "his" place from the beginning. The small-sized kennel (a number 100-series) of the type used for air transportation is ideal for a Cavalier puppy, although the medium size (number 200-series) will be more comfortable when he is an adult. Cavaliers love to snuggle, so purchase two soft, washable blankets or cushions to put in the crate—one to wash, and one to use. Fabric stores are excellent sources for fake sheepskin or plush washable materials for blankets.

Next, create a safe area in the house so that the puppy is out of harm's way if you have to leave him during the day for long periods of time. In preparation for housebreaking, purchase a bottomless playpen, available at dog shows and pet stores, or build a small, fenced enclosure out of rigid garden fencing and stakes. This pen should measure about four feet by four feet and be placed conveniently close to an entry door.

Most importantly, remove any poisonous substances that may be within reach of the puppy inside the house as well as in the garden. Cavalier puppies will put anything in their mouths, including dirt that has been treated with poisonous liquid slug and snail bait or systemic insecticides and fertilizers. Plastic bags can also be extremely hazardous to puppies. In short—anything that is harmful to a small child will be harmful to your new puppy.

Cavaliers of any age should be house pets, but when they are put outside to play, they must be in fenced areas and never be allowed to roam or be

Cavaliers love to snuggle. Benchmark Bunny Hop, owned and bred by Barb Hoorman. Photo by Vicki Roach.

Crates are great for traveling and provide your Cavalier with a feeling of security. Photo by Betty Turner.

kept on a chain or line. They are not an independent breed and do not thrive on being left alone day and night. It is essential that a Cavalier puppy be given quality time if quantity time is not possible.

The Cavalier Puppy's First Day

A Cavalier puppy has a trusting disposition and will soon settle into his new home, but for the first few days he may be lonely for his littermates and the familiarity of his original family. The ideal day to take a puppy home is at the beginning of a weekend, preferably in the morning so that he has the entire day to familiarize himself with his new surroundings before finding himself in the dark of his "first night."

Place the puppy in his kennel by your bedside for the first few nights so if the puppy cries you can comfort him with a hand through the kennel door. The distress of a Cavalier puppy in an unfamiliar home can be acute, and some new owners react to this by taking the puppy to bed with them. While it is desirable for the puppy to be emotionally bonded with you, having him sleep in your bed can cause him to become overly dependent, which in turn can result in a neurotic adult. If the puppy continues to cry after being comforted, it may be necessary to make a trip outside, although this should not be encouraged, as it could become a habit.

Feeding

The breeder should have provided you with a feeding schedule that you should follow as closely as possible. The puppy will be accustomed to being fed at certain times of the day, and the transition period will be easier if he is kept somewhat to this schedule. The puppy may not eat or drink very much for the first few days, but be assured that he will not starve himself. It may just take a little while for him to get back into a routine.

Water may taste and smell different from what the puppy has been used to, so if he is not drinking, bottled water is a temporary alternative. If he is not interested in dry food, put some warm water on it so that it is fragrant, and for a little added incentive, sprinkle some dried, grated parmesan cheese or garlic powder on top. Offering food other than the breeder's recommended puppy diet at this time is not advisable, because it might cause a tummy upset and will also teach the puppy that if he doesn't eat what he is supposed to, something more delicious will be offered. Leaving food out all the time is not a good idea, because this can create a picky eater. Stick to the scheduled mealtime. Feeding the puppy by hand is not a good habit to start either, as once started, it is a hard habit to break. Cow's milk has a high lactose content that will cause diarrhea, so don't give the puppy a bowl of milk to drink. A small amount of goat's milk is acceptable.

A Cavalier puppy is curious and playful. Cosmo and friend, owned by Janet Macdonald. Photo by Janet Macdonald.

Crate Training

Crate (kennel) training will facilitate housebreaking as well as make puppyhood easier to manage. Contrary to popular belief, crate training is not cruel but is one of the most useful tools for raising a puppy.

Start by putting the puppy into his crate with a toy or biscuit and close the door, beginning with a confinement of ten minutes and working up to an hour or two. Don't let him out if he immediately starts crying and scratching at the crate door or he will learn that this is the way to get what he wants. As a general practice, leave the crate door open during the day, so that the puppy can go in and out at will. A two- to four-month-old puppy should never be left in his crate for more than two to three hours at one time, except at night. The puppy's crate is his safe haven and should never be used as punishment. Likewise, children should always be taught to leave a puppy alone when he is in his crate. If you need to be away for long periods, use the safe area described in the previous paragraphs.

The Safe Area

Having an area where it is safe to confine your puppy for several hours will make it less stressful for you and safer for your puppy when you need to leave. A puppy playpen set up in a kitchen or family room is an easy solution, but a laundry room or bathroom will also work as long as the floor is washable. When you use a room instead of a playpen, install a baby gate so that the puppy won't feel shut in and can't learn to scratch at the door. Cavaliers, like all puppies, will chew on anything, so it is essential that there are no electrical outlets or wires within reach and that all potentially toxic medicines or products are safely put away. This includes keeping the lid of the toilet down if automatic toilet-bowl cleaners are used.

The first few nights the Cavalier puppy may be lonely for his littermates. Bramble Knot To Be Forgotten and Bramble Naughty But Nice. Bred by Joy Sims. Photo by Barbara Augello.

Cavaliers respond to love, consistency and praise.
Typical twelve week old puppies. Photo by Vavra

Remove electric cords. If the puppy is kept in the laundry room, encase all reachable connecting wires in a metal flexible casing called armor cable, available at most hardware stores. Spray anything chewable, including the taped electrical wires with chewing deterrent such as Bitter Apple. Whether you use a playpen, the bathroom or the laundry room, put newspaper all over the floor and place the crate with the door fastened open in one corner, along with food, water, and toys. To help the puppy from feeling too alone, keep a radio playing.

Housebreaking

I am amazed when people expect a puppy to become housebroken overnight! Just as a baby has to be potty trained, so does a puppy have to learn that eliminating in the house is unacceptable. A potty-training pen works well for housebreaking. You can easily use an exercise pen, available at dog shows and pet shops, or you can make one. The purpose of this is quite simple. A Cavalier puppy is curious and playful, and when he is put into the garden to eliminate, he will become easily distracted by birds and butterflies and forget to do his business. By putting him in a small pen, there will be no distractions (that he can get at!) and he will learn that if he does his business right away, he will be out of the pen in no time. Take the puppy to his potty pen when he wakes up, after he has eaten, and frequently during the day. At the beginning, watch to see that he eliminates, and when he does, praise him lavishly and let him out of the pen immediately. A kitchen timer works well to remind you that it is time to take a puppy outside; set the timer for an hourly reminder. If the puppy starts sniffing the floor, turning in circles, and squatting, it means that he needs to be taken to the potty pen immediately, even if he is "mid-stream" or has just come in from being outside. Establish a schedule that works for both you and the puppy, and stick to it. Withhold food after five in the evening and limit water intake after that time to help the puppy get through the night without having to be taken outside.

To train the puppy to do his business on command, either whistle or say the same words over and over again while he is eliminating. For instance, you can say "Hurry up." Whistling is how race horses are trained to urinate on command, because the last thing jockeys need is for a horse to come to a grinding halt midcourse to urinate! The puppy will quickly learn to associate the words or the whistle with doing his business and, just like the race horse, will eliminate when he hears the triggering sound.

The idea is to give the puppy as few opportunities as possible to make a mistake. If you are busy and can't watch the puppy, put him in his crate. If you are watching and catch him about to make a mistake or in the middle of one, pick him up, take him outside to his potty pen, and encourage him to finish his business. Leave him in his potty pen for a short time, and when he is finished, take him back into the house. If you find a puddle (or worse!) that happened when you weren't watching, forget it. Don't scold or rub the puppy's nose in it, because puppies can't reason and will just become afraid and confused. Cavaliers respond to love, consistency, and praise rather than to scolding. Train the puppy in this manner and you will be rewarded a thousandfold with a happy, well-adjusted adult.

If paper training is your only option, you will need to train the puppy to eliminate on paper in one place. Place several thicknesses of paper in a suitable spot, then follow the same routine as for the outside potty pen, only take the puppy to his papers instead. There are scented pads on the market that entice a puppy to eliminate on them—a helpful tool for paper training.

A Cavalier puppy should not be given too much freedom too soon. He should be in his crate or safe area when you are not able to watch him until he is at least six months old. Don't allow a puppy the run of the house until he is at least a year old.

Emergency Cleanups

Have something on hand for emergency cleanups, because even the best puppy will make an occasional mistake. White vinegar or soda water will do, and there are also excellent commercial products available to help with stain and odor removal. A hand-held electric carpet cleaner can also be a carpet saver. Cavaliers are innately willing to please, and with consistency and praise,

Never take a puppy that is not fully vaccinated to a park or anywhere else where there have been other dogs. Or squirrels!
CKCSC, USA Champion Chadwick Calamity Jane and friend. Owned by Anne Robins. Photo by Anne Robins

housebreaking should not pose an overwhelming problem.

Vaccinations

Never take a puppy that is not fully vaccinated to a park, a roadside rest stop, or anywhere else where other dogs have been! A puppy should be a minimum of twenty weeks of age prior to exposure to a dog show or to other places where dogs congregate.

Puppies should be vaccinated every three to four weeks through the age of four months, or as recommended by your veterinarian, beginning no later than the eighth week. When you choose a veterinarian, it is helpful, though not necessary, that he or she be familiar with Cavaliers. Give your veterinarian the puppy's shot and worming record supplied by the breeder so that a timely vaccination schedule can be set up. The puppy must at least be vaccinated against Distemper, Parvovirus, Hepatitis, Parainfluenzas I and II, although most veterinarians also include leptospirosis, coronavirus and bordatella in the vaccination schedule. Speak with your veterinarian about possibly vaccinating the puppy without leptospirosis, because this has been known to cause an allergic reaction in Cavaliers, such as a severe swelling of the face. Also discuss the possibility of giving some of the innoculations separately, rather than giving many on the same day. Unless the puppy is going to be in a high-risk situation, to avoid overloading his immune system, it may be safer to use a vaccine with a killed-virus (as opposed to the modified-live virus) whenever possible. This is another option to discuss with your veterinarian. The age of inoculating against Rabies varies from state to state, province to province, and so does the frequency of its administration.

If you ever need to give the puppy pills, use this simple but unorthodox method. Squirt a small amount of whipping cream on the end of a finger, hiding the pill in the cream. Put this into the puppy's mouth—a great treat—and it will make future pill giving easy.

The Importance of Socialization

Although the Cavalier has an inherently good disposition, unless he is properly socialized, he will never reach his full potential. Early socialization can make the difference between a well-adjusted pet and a fearful one. While puppies that are not fully vaccinated should not be walked where there have been other dogs, taking them for a ride in the car and carrying them in town is better than keeping them hidden away. Attend puppy

A well socialized puppy will be allowed to reach his full potential. Sarah and "Petey". Photo by owner.

In pursuit of a dream, Skycrest 'Toria Cross. Demonstrating that the Cavalier does have the true "spaniel" beginnings. Owned by Laura Whittal. Photo by Whittal.

classes when vaccinations have been completed, because these classes build confidence in new situations and provide exposure to other dogs and people.

Swimming

Cavaliers love water. If you have a swimming pool, lake, or river nearby, introduce your puppy to swimming at an early age. Be careful to ensure that the puppy cannot get into a pool area unsupervised, because even though he may know how to swim, he can still drown.

Play Biting

Sometimes Cavalier puppies become rowdy with their owners and may bite playfully. They are not being mean, but those sharp little teeth can hurt. A puppy's dam wouldn't take this type of treatment, and neither should you. The quickest way of putting a stop to this annoying

behavior is to chastise the puppy, just as the dam would do under the same circumstances. Grab the skin on the nape of the neck between your thumb and forefinger, give it a short, sharp shake and sharply say "No!" Repeat as necessary. Then have a chew bone handy to give the puppy instead of your finger. Never, ever hit a puppy.

Have a chew bone handy to give the puppy instead of your finger. "Chelsea", owned by Mr. and Mrs. Stan Regensburg. Photo by Stan Regensburg.

Carnelian Golden Fancy, bred and owned by Victoria Plann. Photo by Victoria Plann.

chapter five
GENERAL CARE

$\mathcal{F}$eeding

There are many commercially prepared dog foods available today, and there are an equal number of differing opinions among the fancy as to which products give the best results. There is some conjecture that Cavaliers are sensitive to artificial preservatives such as BHA, BHT and ethoxyquin, so feeding a diet that is naturally preserved may be prudent. Read labels and discuss choices with your breeder and veterinarian.

An alternative to feeding commercially prepared food is to use one of the published raw

Awaiting his "place at the table". Photo by author.

diets, which consist of organically raised raw meat, grains, and vegetables. Regardless of the method of feeding that you choose, add raw, fresh fruit and vegetables such as carrots, apples, and bananas to the diet. An unpeeled, seeded acorn squash cooked in the microwave for about ten minutes is a special treat, as are baked potatoes, potato skins, and most green vegetables. Our Cavaliers are frequently given whole raw carrots instead of dog biscuits and they love them! One of the best naturally preserved dog foods recommends "setting a place for your dog at the table," a theory to which we have long subscribed.

Food and water bowls are ideally made of stainless steel or glazed crockery. Stainless steel bowls are unbreakable, unlikely to be chewed and are easy to clean. Glazed crockery is a good choice because it is heavy enough so that the dog cannot carry it off, is stable and is easily cleaned. Plastic bowls are less desirable because they are difficult

CKCSC, USA and AKC Ch. Flying Colors Dangerous at Radiant.
Owned by Ann Ray Hutton and Cathy Gish.
Photo by Meager.

Training a Cavalier to wear a snood at mealtimes will keep ear fringes clean. Photo by Vavra.

to get completely clean, can be chewed, and are linked with a contact dermatitis that results in the nose going off color. The best water bowl for a Cavalier is one that is specially designed for a dog with long ears. This bowl, which is broader at the base and narrower at the top, is sometimes called a "spaniel bowl" and is available at most pet stores.

Training a Cavalier to wear a snood at mealtimes will keep ear fringes clean, and will lessen the likelihood of them being chewed off—food dipped ear fringes make tasty morsels! A snood is like a hair net, it fits over the head and keeps the ears tucked neatly out of the way.

Cavaliers are usually enthusiastic about their meals, so it is important to watch their weight to make sure that they don't get fat. When you feed commercial food only, or supplement with food from the table, adjust the amount offered according to your dog's weight, age, and level of physical activity. Don't feed two cups of food a day just because that is what the directions on the side of the bag suggest!

Occasionally a Cavalier will be a picky eater, which can be helped in several ways. Competition at the food bowl often works when there is more than one dog in the household, but when there is only one, it may be necessary to resort to more creative tactics. Have a regular schedule for feeding and offer food only then, don't leave food out for free choice. Have the food available only until the dog stops eating, then pick it up and don't offer it again until the next scheduled feeding time. Another option is to try changing the food offered, but a sudden change to a completely different type of food can cause

Grooming is made easy with the proper tools. Photo by Vavra

Competition at the food bowl often works when there is more than one dog in the household. Photo by author.

diarrhea, so begin with mixing the new variety with the old. Moistening the food with warm water and sprinkling dried parmesan cheese on top, or mixing in some canned food or even a little cooked meat or chicken with the normal ration may be enough to tempt the picky eater, but whatever you do, do not fall into the habit of feeding the dog by hand, as once this is started, it is a very difficult habit to break. Don't worry, the dog will not starve himself! Appetite enchancers are available from the veterinarian or from catalogs.

Puppies should be fed three times daily. An adult Cavalier's food ration can be divided into two meals if desired—one morning, one evening. It is very important to keep plenty of clean, fresh water available at all times.

Grooming
Equipment and Supplies

Grooming tools for the Cavalier consist of a grooming table, a waterproof apron, a blow dryer and towels, nail clippers, cauterizing powder, a toothbrush, dog toothpaste, cotton balls, detanglers, shampoo, conditioner, brushes, combs, blunt-ended scissors or electric clippers, mineral oil, and finishing spray (optional).

There are many pet shampoos designed to fit individual needs. These are available from pet stores, catalogs and dog shows. Flea shampoo, conditioning shampoo, stain-removing shampoo, and the list goes on!

There are three types of brushes that are indispensable for keeping the Cavalier coat well groomed—an oblong pin brush, a slicker brush, and a bristle brush. The pin brush has metal pins coming out of a rubber pad and is used for general purposes. The slicker brush, used to gently tease out knots and tangles, consists of wire pins bent at an angle half way down the pin's shaft. For a Cavalier, choose a brush with pins that flex easily and that do not feel harsh when pressed against the palm of the hand. The bristle brush is used primarily to clean the coat and bring out its sheen. I have a friend who gives the final glow to the coat by using a shoe-polishing brush!

The best comb for grooming the Cavalier is an all-purpose or "greyhound" comb, which has wide-spaced tines at one end and more finely spaced tines at the other. A mat comb is also a useful tool for cutting through those mats that are impossible to pull apart by hand.

Pin brush:	PSI Oblong for brushing out long furnishings (ears, tail, chest).
Slicker brush:	Two types: Warner (for removing dead undercoat and for drying thick, curly ears and furnishings); Doggie Man (a softer, gentler type for finer, more delicate furnishings).
Combs:	The traditional English greyhound or one of the newer Japanese round backed combs.
Shampoo:	White on White; Ultra White Stain Removing Shampoo
De-tangler and Coat protector:	Ice on Ice; The Stuff
Rinseless Shampoo:	Show Off; Self-Rinse Plus
Coat Conditioner:	Vellus Satin Cream; Pro-Gro
Dryer:	Super Duck
Under Eye Stain:	Diamond Eye
Lead:	Slide lead (collar and lead all in one) and Resco or chain and snap lead
Carpet Stain Remover:	Nature's Miracle
Dietary Supplement:	The Missing Link
Wormer:	Panacur
Ear cleaner:	Epiotic
Eye cleaner:	Occuclear
High calorie paste:	Nutri-Cal
Styptic powder:	Quik Stop
Airline carrier:	Sherpa Bag (large)
Kennel:	Vari Kennel #200
Bed:	Wally Bed
Chew Toys:	Booda Velvet Bones Jawrobic by Kong Toys

The hair between the pads on the underside of the foot should be trimmed regularly. Photo by Vavra.

nominal fee. If the sacs are full, they can easily be felt as small firm lumps on either side of the anus, at the five and seven o'clock position. With your thumb and forefinger, take hold of the skin on either side of the anus where indicated, then push in and squeeze. Watch out! The contents can come out terriffic force. Next, clip the toenails, taking care not to cut them too closely. (The vein in the quick will bleed heavily if the nail is cut too short, but this can easily be stopped with the application of cauterizing powder, to the nail tip). The hair between the pads on the underside of the foot should be trimmed regularly with either blunt-ended scissors or electric clippers. Be careful not to cut the pads! Lastly, apply mineral oil or Tieline in the eyes to prevent irritation from shampoo.

Before starting, put on a waterproof apron. The place to begin wetting the Cavalier will depend on the reason for the bath. If you are giving him a flea bath, it is better to start at the head and work toward the tail. The head, neck and rear are usually the areas of heaviest flea infestation, so first apply the flea shampoo around the neck and hindquarters. This will stop the fleas from escaping to the rest of the body. Otherwise, there will be less resistance from the dog if you first spray the water on his back, working forward toward the head.

Wet the dog thoroughly and completely with warm water, spraying in the direction the hair grows, not against the grain. Cavaliers have fine hair, so do not use a forceful spray nozzle because it tends to cause breakage. Make a good lather and

Bathing

Put your Cavalier on the grooming table and brush out all knots and mats in the coat, because these can become difficult or impossible to pull apart and remove once they are wet. Knots will be more easily removed if first sprayed with a detangler. Next, clean the teeth with a toothpaste for dogs, applied with a soft toothbrush. Gently clean the ears removing dirt and wax buildup with a cotton ball and a solution made especially for this purpose, such as Epiotic. Check to see if the anal sacs need expressing. Emptying the sacs is not a difficult procedure, although not the most pleasant of tasks, and one a veterinarian will do for a massage gently through the coat, never scrubbing, because any rough treatment of the hair during bathing or drying will result in breakage. Rinse thoroughly and repeat. Mix the conditioner and water as directed on the bottle and place the solution in a plastic bowl. Then dip in the ears, followed by the tail. Distribute the rest of the conditioner over the body, let it sit for a few minutes, and rinse thoroughly. Conditioners that you can either leave in or spray on which are especially helpful in dry climates or where there is a lot of static electricity.

Blot out excessive water with a towel, then dry thoroughly with the blow dryer set on warm, not hot. For dogs with sensitive skin due to allergies, use only the cool setting. Brush out the ears, the chest, the tail and the body. When the coat is thoroughly dry, spritz it with a finishing spray if desired.

Geriatric Care

Many Cavaliers live to be twelve years old and older, although the average lifespan is less.

Dogs are generally considered to be seniors when they are seven years old. The first step to take when your Cavalier is becoming a senior, is to feed him accordingly. If you are using a commercial food, use one specifically formulated for older dogs that contains less protein, fat, and salt and fewer calories than those made for younger, more active dogs. The amount offered of any food should depend on the ability of the dog to maintain a proper weight.

Make sure that your senior Cavalier's teeth are clean and that none are loose or decayed. Only if absolutely necessary, have a veterinarian clean and remove some teeth under an anesthetic. If the teeth are very dirty, veterinarians recommend that oral antibiotics be given before dental work is done and that the antibiotics be continued for several days afterwards.

Bedding should be soft with plenty of padding to ease old bones, and it goes without saying that the bed should be in a warm, draft free area of the house. Special heating pads are available for pets, the covers of which are removable for laundering.

Older Cavaliers should still have moderate exercise, because even though they are content to spend much time asleep, it is healthier for them to have some activity. In poor weather, the use of a warm sweater or raincoat will help keep them warm and dry. It is essential to dry an older Cavalier thoroughly after a wet outing.

Continue to groom on a regular basis, watching his general condition and looking for unusual lumps or hair loss. Trim nails frequently, because the less active dog will not wear them down naturally. This is also true regarding foot fringes, which can become excessive due to inactivity—causing the dog some difficulty in walking.

Deafness is often part of the aging process. If you suspect that your Cavalier may be going deaf, start teaching him hand signals. This is much easier to accomplish while the dog still has some hearing, although it can be done when the dog is already deaf. Of course, if your Cavalier is like many of ours, he will have selective hearing, so you do have to be able to differentiate between the two!

Saying Good-bye

The hardest part of being a responsible dog owner is being able to say good-bye when the time is right. Don't let your Cavalier suffer because you don't have the courage to put him to sleep. You must love your dog enough to let him go. It takes an enormous amount of courage to hold a beloved pet in your arms while he dies, but there is some consolation in knowing that the last thing he knows is the sound of your voice and the touch of your hand.

Canadian Champion Charlemere Wishing Star
at age 11, owned by Angela Thomas.
Photo by Thomas.

Canadian Champion Amantra Pinball Wizard
at age 13, owned by Olivia Darbyshire and Louise Pearce.
Photo by Vavra.

Laughing Sailor's Serenade, CD, shown winning
Best Veteran in Show at the 1997 CKCSC, USA
National Specialty under breed specialist judge
Joyce Boardman. Owned by Jim Hoorman.
Photo by Digital Artistry.

Mr. and Mrs. Lou Rukeyser and Cavaliers. Photo by Bob Capazzo Photography.

chapter six

KEEPING YOUR CAVALIER HEALTHY

*P*ossibly the most important relationship for any dog owner is the one with his veterinarian. Look around your area for a good small-animal veterinarian even before you bring your dog home. If possible, obtain a recommendation from another owner or breeder of Cavaliers so that you know if the vet has experience with the breed. Within a few days after purchase, have your puppy or adult dog examined and any records from his previous owner recorded

CKCSC, USA Champion Flying Colors Forever in Love, owned and bred by Cathy Gish. Photo by Jan Wendell Photographic Portraits.

with your clinic.

It is important that you keep a record of your dog's normal signs so that you and your veterinarian can more readily recognize illness. For example, a dog's normal temperature can range from 100.5 to 102 degrees, with the average being 101.5. Having a record of your dog's normal temperature and pulse can be important when he is showing early symptoms of illness. Common signs that should not be ignored are listlessness, dull or dry coat, runny eyes or nose, coughing, sneezing, excessive scratching, frequent or painful urination, vomiting, diarrhea, stiffness or a higher-than-normal temperature. Loss of appetite, change of habits or lethargy should also be noted.

After the initial series of puppy shots, annual boosters for distemper, hepatitis, parvovirus, and other diseases are recommended by veterinarians. Rabies vaccinations are usually good for three years, but state, provincial and local licensing laws may require annual or biannual boosters. When you take your Cavalier for puppy shots, you have the perfect time to ask about heartworm or flea preventatives, discuss any concerns or health-related questions, or take a stool sample to have it tested for parasites. Just as with humans, an annual exam can uncover medical conditions before they become serious or life-threatening.

Every dog owner should have an emergency first-aid kit. First aid is almost identical for man and dog. If you don't have the slightest notion how to proceed, at least don't panic and don't frighten the dog!

Vaccinations

Cavalier puppies should be vaccinated every three weeks, with the recommended ages being from six weeks through four months. Adults are given annual boosters or should have their titers checked by the veterinarian to ensure their level of immunity against life-threatening diseases is sufficient.

Anal Glands

If you see your Cavalier "scooting" his bottom on the floor, it is very likely that the anal sacs, or scent glands, need emptying. Some Cavaliers need to have these glands emptied more frequently than others. The contents of anal sacs are foul smelling and often come out with considerable force, squirting in all directions. Because of this, anal glands should be emptied just before bathing begins. If anal sacs become impacted, veterinary help is necessary because infection will follow and the dog can become quite ill. Some vet-erinarians advocate surgical removal of anal sacs if the problem is a recurrent one. See Chapter 5 in the section on grooming for directions on emptying the anal sacs.

Blood Platelets

Cavaliers have larger platelets than most other breeds of dog, so special laboratory procedures need to be used when evaluating them.

Coughs

An occasional cough is normal, a persistent cough is not. A virus such as kennel cough, a throat irritation or heart disease are possible causes. Veterinary advice should be sought.

Diarrhea

There are many causes of diarrhea, from mild stomach upsets to serious diseases such as parvovirus or coronavirus. Like children, Cavaliers will put almost anything in their mouths, some of which can cause diarrhea and vomiting. Withhold all food for twenty-four hours. If the diarrhea persists or there is blood in the stool, consult your vet.

CKCSC, USA and Canadian Champion Wyndcrest Tiny Bubbles, owned and bred by Mr. and Mrs. Harold Letterly. Photo by Vavra.

USEFUL HOUSEHOLD MEDICATIONS FOR DOGS		
Medication	**Dosage**	**Problem**
Buffered aspirin	.5 mg. per lb. every 12 hours	anti-inflammatory, pain relief
NO Tylenol	NO Tylenol	NO Tylenol
Benadryl	2 mg. per lb. every 8 hours	allergies, stings
Dramamine	no more than 50 mg. every 8 hrs	car sickness
Peroxide 3%	10 ml. orally every 15 mins.	to induce vomiting
Kaopectate	1 ml. per lb. every 2 hours	for diarrhea
Pepto Bismal	1 tsp. per 5 lbs. every 6 hours	diarrhea and vomiting

Ears

While Cavaliers are not as prone to ear infections as some other spaniels, regularly check the inside of the ears to see that they are clean and free from infection or parasites. Frequent head shaking can indicate a foreign body or other irritant such as wax build up, ear mites or yeast infection. If you suspect a foreign body, get veterinary attention as soon as possible. Veterinary care is necessary but not an emergency if you suspect an infection or parasite.

Deafness can be either genetic or acquired. A blow to the head or a history of ear infections can result in acquired deafness. Old age can be another cause, with onset being gradual, usually around ten years old. When living with a dog that is hard of hearing, two dogs are better than one, as one will take cues from the other. Dogs tend to hear better at higher pitches, hard sounds are better than soft ones, and short words are easier for the hard of hearing dog to understand, so when giving commands, speak accordingly. Some deaf dogs will snap if they are suddenly surprised or awakened, so caution may be appropriate with young children.

Eyes

Cavaliers have large eyes in shallow sockets, easily irritated by dust and wind. Dampen a cotton wool ball with warm water or a boric acid solution and wipe over the eye to remove any dirt or debris. If the eyes are irritated, some over-the-counter preparations for human eye discomfort can be used as a temporary treatment, but if irritation persists, see a veterinarian. Tearing can be caused by teething, allergies, infections elsewhere in the body and plugged tearducts. Excessive tearing can cause a red stain under the eye. This stain can be removed by applying a product specifically made for the purpose, available at most pet stores. The accompanying musty odor is caused by bacteria. The practice of using antibiotics to lessen under-eye discoloration is not advisable unless under the direction of a veterinarian. For a description of the more common eye problems affecting the Cavalier, see Chapter Ten: Inherited Health Disorders.

Feet and Nails

Nails should be kept short and the hair on the underside of the pad should be clipped. Nails that are not kept clipped can get caught in ears fringes, cause the dog to have splayed feet, to become down in the pasterns and interfere with movement. Many Cavaliers have had their dewclaws removed, but if these are still present, remember to keep them clipped also. Keep the hair trimmed between the pads on the underside of the foot to prevent painful hair balls from forming. This hair can form hard lumps, causing your Cavalier discomfort.

Heart Disease

The health issue of primary concern in Cavaliers is Mitral Valve Disease, a disease that veterinary cardiologists agree is probably genetically transmitted. Little is known about the disease at this time, other than that there are no bloodlines that are known to be free of it.

Simply put, mitral valve disease results in a leaky valve that allows blood to flow back into the heart. The heart enlarges, and eventually congestive heart failure develops. The acquired condition, endocarditis, is a bacterial growth on the mitral valve, and while it is not hereditary, the end result is the same as the inherited endocardiosis. Some veterinarians recommend that Cavaliers be treated with antibiotics before and after having their teeth cleaned as a preventative measure against this condition.

While there is no cure for heart disease, prescription medications (Lasix, Digoxin, Vasotec) are available that will keep the dog comfortable and perhaps will enable him to live longer than he otherwise might. Other treatments include a low sodium diet, maintaining proper weight and continuing moderate exercise. Many Cavaliers do live happy, normal lives with a heart murmur.

Some cardiologists say that antioxidant vitamins and products such as Co Enzyme-Q (see Immune System) may help forestall heart disease by boosting the immune system. This is a new idea which has not been proven, but can do no harm, so is worth pursuing.

Hernias

Umbilical hernias are not uncommon in Cavaliers but usually resolve spontaneously and seldom need repair. See Hernias in the chapter Raising a Litter of Cavalier Puppies.

Hip Dysplasia

Canine Hip Dysplasia (CHD) is the most common inherited orthopedic problem seen in dogs, and it is more troublesome in large and giant breeds than it is in the medium-size and toy breeds. CHD is when the ball and socket of the hip joint do not fit properly, which can lead to arthritis and lameness. The dog may have an irregular gait or have difficulty rising to a standing position. Treatment involves rest, medication, and possible surgery. Due to their small size, Cavaliers afflicted with CHD may never exhibit any signs of the disease.

Hypoglycemia

Hypoglycemia (low blood sugar) is not uncommon in Cavalier puppies under six months of age. Puppies can have glucose depletion much more quickly than adults, the usual cause of which is an incomplete development of diverse metabolic pathways. Puppies have relatively large brains in ratio to the size of their livers, so they are always closer to glucose deficiency than adults. Symptoms include lack of coordination, weakness, and seizures. Seizures usually follow a period of high activity, and are recognized by foaming at the mouth and having an involuntary bowel movement. Cavalier puppies usually outgrow this condition by six months, unless there is a deeper underlying problem. Caloric intake must be supplemented

*CKCSC, USA and Canadian Champion
Kindrum Marcus of Crossbow.
Owned by David and Wesely Schiffman. Photo by Meager.*

The Cavalier is a hardy breed, and with proper diet and exercise should lead a healthy life, as do the Laughing Cavaliers pictured above. Photo by the author.

until normal pathways are working, which is the reason puppies should be fed three to four times daily through at least four months of age.

Hypothyroidism

Hypothyroidism (underactive thyroid), occurs occasionally among Cavaliers. Symptoms may include obesity, dull hair coat, hair loss, constant infections, laziness, low sperm counts in males, "missed" pregnancies, small litter sizes or whelping complications, but most importantly hypothyroidism disrupts the immune system. A simple and inexpensive set of tests called a thyroid panel (T3 and T4) should be run by your veterinarian. After thyroid supplementation is regulated, improvement is usually dramatic within a few weeks with correct dosage.

Immune System

For general good health, keep the immune system healthy. Antioxidant vitamins E and C,

products such as Co Enzyme-Q (reputed to increase cellular energy) and Blue Green Algae (a simple, accessible form of amino acids, rich in macro and trace minerals) are recommended by veterinarians. Vitamin E is dosed at 400 units daily and Vitamin C at 500 units daily.

Noses

Hyperkeratosis is when the skin of the nose becomes rough to the touch and appears cracked and dry. Keep the nose lubricated with mineral oil or vaseline, and if there is any infection present, treat the nose with a topical antibiotic such as Neomycin.

Obesity

Cavaliers should not be allowed to become overweight. Their ribs should be easily felt but not show too obviously. Obesity is recognized by the rib cage not being visible when the Cavalier moves; there is a lack of "waist."

Parasites

Some of the worms and parasites that can cause stomach upsets are tapeworms, roundworms, hookworms, whip worms and the protozoans coccidia, and giardia. Perhaps the safest and most effective dewormer is fenbendazole (Panacur), which will rid the dog of most of the worms mentioned, and will also treat giardia. Dogs that are on heartworm preventative, (Heart-guard or Interceptor), will automatically be protected against the mentioned worms except tapeworms.

Worms

Tapeworms and roundworms are the most common type seen in the dog's stool but do not rely on seeing them if an infestation is suspected, because they can be overlooked. Tapeworm segments, which are white, flat, and blunt-ended, look like kernels of rice around the anus when dry. Roundworms are white, thin, and pointed at both ends, and resemble a small spring or coil in the stool. A puppy should have a stool sample checked by his

The picture of health. Metcroft Tyler in enthusiastic pursuit. Owned and bred by Rosemary Dunstall. Photo by Dunstall.

EMERGENCY FIRST AID KIT

The following items should be ready in case of an emergency:

- Veterinarian's phone number
- Peroxide
- Sterile bandages
- Thermometer
- Scissors
- Baby aspirin
- Silver nitrate or ferric subsulfate (cauterizing powder)
- Tweezers
- Ear cleaner
- Antihistamine
- Antiseptic solution
- Saline solution and syringe (eye wash)
- Diarrhea medication
- Electrolyte solution
- Tube of high calorie dietary supplement (such as Nutri-Cal)

Poison Control Hotline
1-800-548-2423 in the USA
1-800-567-8911 in Canada

---

veterinarian on his first visit, and on a regular schedule as advised. Adults should have a stool sample run annually unless worms are suspected, the signs of which include a dull coat, diarrhea or a slimy mucus in the stool, rubbing his bottom on the ground, and a general lack of "bloom."

Coccidiosis and Giardiasis

It is not unusual for a puppy to "break" with coccidiosis when he leaves home due to stress. This does not mean that the puppy has been raised in dirty conditions! Diarrhea with blood in it is usually the result coccidiosis or the water borne giardiasis. Coccidiosis is usually treated with sulfadimethoxine (Albon) for several days, and giardiasis with metronidazole (Flagyl) or fenbendazole (Panacur)

Fleas

Cavaliers can develop a flea-bite allergy, that causes red, itchy skin. Fleas can be kept under control by using one of the monthly oral anti-flea preparations, such as Program, which arrests development of pre-adult fleas through insect growth hormone regulators. Spot treatments such as Advantage, Frontline, and Breakthrough kill adult fleas, as do topical dips, sprays, and shampoos. Be cautious when using some shampoos and flea dips because they can be quite toxic.

Heartworm

Heartworm, which is transmitted by mosquitoes, is a type of roundworm that lives in the bloodstream. Cavaliers living in an area where heartworm is present must be treated with preventative medication, (such as Heartgurad, Interceptor or Filaribits.) If untreated, heartworm can lead to congestive heart failure and death.

Cheyletiella

A tiny mite called cheyletiella, or walking dandruff, is surprisingly quite common, particularly in puppies and young dogs. The dog will scratch for no apparent reason, until the owner notices dandruff, particularly over the dog's head, neck, and back. Cheyletiella should be suspected if the owner notices bites anywhere material is tight against his own body. Dandruff scrapings examined under a microscope by a veterinarian will identify the mite. As a remedy, discuss the use of Ivomectin with your veterinarian. Other suggestions are dips and insecticide shampoos.

Canadian Champion Cinola Blondie, 1992 Canadian National Specialty winner, owned by Dorcas Mycock. Photo by Mycock.

Ticks

After an outing in long grass or wooded areas where ticks might be present, check the dog for ticks, and if found, carefully remove, destroy, disinfect the site of the tick, than wash your hands thoroughly. In some areas, ticks can carry a serious illness called Lyme disease. If you live or are vacationing in one of these areas, ask your veterinarian about the advisability of a preventative innoculation.

Patellar Luxation

A common fault in all small breeds, patellar dislocation or luxation occurs in the back leg when the groove carrying the tendon in the knee is too shallow, causing the kneecap to slip. When displacement of the knee occurs, the dog can experience considerable pain. Usually the first signs appear at about ten months to a year of age, when the dog will suddenly cry out and start carrying his back leg. If this happens, take hold of the leg above the knee and straighten it, thus putting the tendon temporarily back into its groove. Other symptoms are a limp or standing with the hocks out and the toes pointed in. Treatment involves surgery.

Poison

If you suspect that your Cavalier has swallowed poison, act immediately, because time is critical. Immediately call your vet or the

National Animal Poison Control Center
In the USA :1-800-548-2423
and in Canada 1-800-567-8911

Get to your veterinarian as soon as possible. If inducing vomiting is called for, give your dog one teaspoon of household peroxide, and if this brings no results, give two more teaspoons in half an hour. Ipecac or table salt will also induce vomiting.

Seizures

Hereditary epilepsy is thankfully uncommon in the Cavalier. "Fly-catchers Syndrome," while rare, is the most frequent type of epilepsy seen in the breed and can be recognized by the dog snapping at imaginary flies or constantly chasing his tail. A blow to the head, a viral infection, poisoning, adverse reaction to a vaccination or a brain tumor are possible causes of seizures. The onset of genetically transmitted epilepsy usually occurs between the ages of one and four years of age. Seizures in puppies less than six months of age are often caused by hypoglycemia, (discussed earlier in this chapter) which is common in puppies of all toy breeds.

Snorting

The characteristic "Cavalier snort" is caused by an elongated soft palate. There will be a sudden intake of breath, accompanied by a loud snorting sound. Then the dog will tuck up in the middle and usually stand still or walk slowly until the spasm passes. Often associated with excitement, snorting is not dangerous. It can usually be stopped by placing your hand over his nostrils, momentarily restricting the intake of air.

Stings

Cavaliers do love to snap at insects as they fly by. It is as well that they are rarely successful at catching them, because a sting in the mouth or throat by a wasp or bee can be life-threatening, requiring immediate medical attention. Although bee stings are not usually dangerous, occasionally an allergic reaction can result; therefore it is a good idea to have an antihistamine or Benadril on hand.

Teeth

Dogs have forty-two permanent teeth that are usually visible between sixteen and thirty weeks of age. Check Cavalier puppies regularly to be sure that every milk tooth has fallen out when the adult tooth is in place. Sometimes there will be both a milk tooth and an adult tooth side by side or one tooth behind the other. In this case, the milk tooth must be extracted, because if it is left in place, a displaced permanent tooth may result.

Canadian and AKC Champion Kewpy's Cascade of Cambridge, owned by Elaine Mitchell and Karen Wills. Photo by Missy Yuhl.

Some Cavaliers get tartar buildup on their teeth more frequently than others. Daily brushing with a canine toothpaste or warm water with a few drops of peroxide added will reduce the incidence of tooth decay and gum disease. Raw beef marrowbones of good size or rawhide bones (never chicken or pork) are good to keep gums exercised. Annual scaling of your Cavalier's teeth by a veterinarian will help keep the breath sweet and prevent gum disease. Many veterinarians put Cavaliers on an antibiotic before deep cleaning their teeth as a precaution against bacteria migrating into the bloodstream. Cavaliers with heart disease should not be put under an anesthetic without careful consideration.

Cavalier puppies should be vaccinated every three weeks. Benchmark Lil' Miss Marker and Benchmark Spring Rainbow CD. Photo by Vicki Roach.

E.T. "Bud" Warden and Tiger Mountain Joanne winning at the Canadian Cavalier Booster Show, 1982. Photo by Warden.

THE HUMAN AGE OF YOUR CAVALIER

Dog	Human
6 mos.	10 yrs
1 yr	.16
2	.25
3	.29
4	.32
5	.37
6	.40
7	.44
8	.47
9	.52
10	.55
11	.60
12	.64
13	.68
14	.72
15	.77
16	.80
17	.85
18	.88
19	.92

Group winning Canadian Champion Salador Coogan, J.W.
with owner/handler L. Garrett Lambert and judge Nigel Aubrey Jones.
Photo by Alex Smith Photography.

chapter seven

UNDERSTANDING THE BREED STANDARD

*A*ll purebred dogs have a standard of excellence that is established by the parent breed club and its governing body (i.e.: the American or Canadian Kennel Club and in the USA also the CKCSC, USA). This standard becomes the guideline for conformation judges and breeders. A Breed Standard creates a word picture of the ideal male and female dog of that particular breed and describes their function and the way in which they move. It also defines the basic character of the breed. The Breed Standard is the blueprint of a breed and is the final authority for its evaluation. Whether or not you plan to breed or show, it behooves all fanciers to read and study their breed's Standard. Every purebred Cavalier, including one chosen solely for companionship, should look and act in a manner characteristic of the breed.

If you plan to show your Cavalier, it is essential that he represent the Standard as closely as possible. It is especially important that he not have any disqualifying faults. Read the various Standards carefully and study the illustrations until you have in your mind the picture of your ideal Cavalier. Only then should you embark on a quest to find that right dog. When evaluating a puppy, keep in mind that Cavaliers go through many changes. Very few are glamorous puppies or do top winning from the puppy classes. Each line and each breeder's family of dogs develop and change at their own particular rate, known intimately to the breeder. Mouths change greatly, as do toplines and ear sets. The novice breeder would be wise to

put their faith in an experienced breeder as a mentor rather than floundering unguided and gathering myriad conflicting opinions. A qualified breeder, well versed in type and experienced in the breed, can overlook minor imperfections in order to maintain breed type or to incorporate into their line a desired but presently lacking trait, such as eye, coat, substance and size.

There are no "perfect" dogs, but every breeder must protect the future of his or her breed by breeding only those specimens that excel in structure, health and temperament, and that are characteristic of the breed in every way.

CKCSC, USA and AKC Champion Pinecrest Kiss Me Kate. Owned and bred by Ted and Mary Grace Eubank. Top Cavalier bitch for 1996. Photo by Gay Glazbrook.

Breed Standards for the Cavalier King Charles Spaniel

The American Kennel Club

I. GENERAL APPEARANCE

The Cavalier King Charles Spaniel is an active, graceful, well-balanced toy spaniel, very gay and free in action; fearless and sporting in character, yet at the same time gentle and affectionate. It is this typical gay temperament, combined with true elegance and royal appearance which are of paramount importance in the breed. Natural appearance with no trimming, sculpting or artificial alteration is essential to breed type.

The Canadian Kennel Club

An active, graceful, well-balanced dog; very gay and free in action.

The Cavalier King Charles Spaniel Club, USA

An active, graceful, well balanced dog, very gay and free in action. Fearless and sporting in character, yet at the same time gentle and affectionate.

Discussion: A Cavalier should show an enthusiasm for life, characterized by a buoyant attitude and the happily waving tail. Action should not be stilted, but should be free and ground covering. The Cavalier is an athletic breed and should be shown in top physical condition. General carriage should be elegant. This is a royal toy spaniel, and it's demeanor and bearing should indicate such.

II. SIZE, PROPORTION, SUBSTANCE

Size: Height twelve to thirteen inches at the withers; weight proportionate to height, between thirteen and eighteen pounds. A small well balanced dog within these weights is desirable, but these are ideal heights and weights and slight variations are permissible. *Proportion:* The body approaches squareness, yet if measured from point of shoulder to point of buttock, is slightly longer than the height at the withers. The height from the withers to the elbow is approximately equal to the height from the elbow to the ground. Weedy and coarse specimens are to be equally penalized.

Height 12–13 inches (30–33 cm). Weight proportionate to height between 12–18 pounds (5–8 kg). Slight variations permissible. Penalize only in comparison with equal quality, appearance and type. A small, well-balanced dog well between these measurements is desirable.

Height twelve to thirteen inches at the withers. Weight proportionate to height, between thirteen and eighteen pounds. These are ideal heights and weights. Slight variations are permissible, and a dog should be penalized only in comparison with one of equal general appearance, type and quality. The weedy specimen is as much to penalized as the oversized one.

Discussion: The Cavalier is first and foremost a toy breed and every effort must be given to promote those specimens within the limits of the Standard. A well-balanced Cavalier should be slightly longer from withers to point of buttocks than from withers to ground. Leeway should be given to those that exceed either end of the scale only if they are of such quality to warrant consideration. Size and substance are not the same. It is equally possible to have an oversized weedy dog as it is to have an undersized coarse and common one. A balanced dog, well within the size variations, is the ideal.

The American Kennel Club	The Canadian Kennel Club	The Cavalier King Charles Spaniel Club, USA

III. HEAD

Proportionate to size of dog, appearing neither too large or too small for the body. Expression: The sweet, gentle melting expression is an important breed characteristic.

Eyes: Large round, but not prominent and set well apart; color a warm, very dark brown, giving a lustrous limpid look. Rims dark. There should be a cushioning under the eyes which contributes to the soft expression. Faults: Small, almond-shaped, prominent or light eyes; white surrounding ring.

Eyes: should be large, round and set well apart; color a warm, dark brown giving a lustrous, limpid look. Faults include white ring surrounding the iris and bulging eyes.

Eyes: Large, round and set well apart: color a warm very dark brown, giving a lustrous limpid look. There should be a slight cushioning under the eyes, which contributes much to the sweet, gentle expression characteristic of the breed. Faults: Small, almond-shaped, prominent or light eyes. White surrounding ring.

Correct Eye	*Light Eye*	*White Surrounding Ring*	*Almond Eye*

Discussion: The eyes are the single most important feature of the Cavalier's appearance. The countenance of a Cavalier should be gentle and welcoming, not startled, mean, or hard. There should be no white showing in the eyes. While the eyes should be large, round, full and widely spaced, they must be placed in the head, not on the head causing them to be bulging and staring. Softness of expression is paramount. It is said that the eye is the window to the soul, and nowhere is this more true than with the Cavalier. Once you have seen the correct eye and expression, nothing else will suffice. Cushioning refers to the padding on either side of the muzzle, below the eye, which gives the muzzle a soft, round appearance. Too much cushioning will give a coarse look, while too little will lend itself to an overall snipey look to the face.

Ears: Set high, but not close on top of the head. Leather long with plenty of feathering and wide enough so that when the dog is alert, the ears fan slightly forward to frame the face.

Ears: set high, but not close to the top of the head. Leather long with plenty of silky feathering, and wide enough so that when the dog is alert, the ears fan slightly forward to frame the face.

Ears: Set high, but not close, on top of the head. Leather long with plenty of feathering and wide enough so that when the dog is alert, the ears fan slightly forward to frame the face.

Discussion: Ears should never be low set, as are those of Cocker Spaniels. Ear fringes should be long and full. Ears are mobile and are a barometer of the dog's moods. Beautiful fully feathered ears are a distinctive feature of the breed.

Skull: Slightly rounded, but without dome or peak; it should appear flat because of the high placement of the ears. Stop is moderate, neither filled nor deep.

Head almost flat between the ears, without dome. Stop shallow; length from the base of the stop to tip of nose about 1 1/2 inches (4 cm). Nostrils should be well developed and the pigment black.

The skull is slightly rounded, but without dome or peak. It should appear flat because of the high placement of the ears.

Discussion: The head of the Cavalier is of particular importance. The skull of the Cavalier must not have any tendency to being domed. A Cavalier in repose will drop his ears, making the slight roundness of the skull more apparent. The flat appearance of the head is due to the set of the ears in alert position. The bones on the side of the head by the ears must be flat. Any bulging, termed cheekiness, leads to coarseness and an overdone appearance. It must be noted that the head should be in balance with the body, as nothing looks more peculiar than a pin headed dog. It is important to note that many terms in the Standard are comparative or interpretative. In regard to the head, the breed that the Cavalier is most frequently compared to is the English Toy Spaniel. Thus, a moderate stop means moderate when compared to an English Toy Spaniel, not when compared to a Brittany or English Cocker Spaniel.

The American Kennel Club	The Canadian Kennel Club	The Cavalier King Charles Spaniel Club, USA
Muzzle: Full muzzle, slightly tapered. Length from base of stop to tip of nose is about one and one-half inches. Face well filled below eyes. Any tendency towards snipeyness undesirable.	*Muzzle:* Tapered. Lips well covering but not hound-like. There should be cushioning beneath the eyes, which contributes much to the sweet, gentle expression characteristic of the breed.	Well tapered mouth level, lips well covering. Faults: Sharp, pointed or snipey muzzle. Full or pendulous lips. Flesh marks, i.e. patches of pink pigment showing through hair on muzzle.

Discussion: The muzzle should be tapered but not have a pointed look to it, giving the appearance of having sucked a lemon. Neither should lips be like those of a Saint Bernard or Bloodhound. The lip line should be clean, covering the lower jaw. When viewed from the front, the muzzle should be round and full, not drooping and not pinched. A line drawn from the center of each eye to the center of the nose, and a line drawn from the center of the eye to the center of the other eye—should be an equilateral triangle.

Nose pigment uniformly black without flesh marks and nostrils well developed. Lips well developed but not pendulous giving a clean finish. Faults: Sharp or pointed muzzles.

Nose: There should be a shallow stop, and the length from the base of stop to tip of nose should be at least one and one-half inches. Nostrils should be well developed and the pigment uniformly black. Faults: Putty or "dudley" noses (off-color) and white patches on the nose are serious faults, as are small, pinched nostrils.

Discussion: The length of the nose (muzzle) should be neither overly short nor overly long. The stop should not be deep, as in that of the King Charles Spaniel (English Toy), or filled, as in that of the English Cocker Spaniel. The stop is moderate in depth and slightly sloping, and the eyebrows are well defined. While the CKCSC, USA Standard says that the length of the nose shall be at least one and one-half inches, this will vary with the size of the dog. Many breeders feel that the proportion should be two-thirds skull to one-third muzzle. A shorter Cavalier will have a correspondingly smaller muzzle. Nose color may vary slightly with hormonal influences and weather but should generally be black, with no brown or pink tinges. White patches on puppies will often fill in with age.

Good ear placement. Correct length of stop. Eyes slightly too small—giving mean expression.

Stop too shallow—snipey muzzle. Eyes correct—round and dark.

Ear set too low—domed skull. White surrounding ring in eyes. Pendoulous lips.

The American Kennel Club	The Canadian Kennel Club	The Cavalier King Charles Spaniel Club, USA

Bite: A perfect, regular, and complete scissors bite is preferred, i.e. the upper teeth closely overlapping the lower teeth and set square to the jaws. Faults: Undershot bite, weak or crooked teeth, crooked jaws.

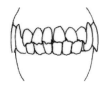

Mouth: teeth strong and even, preferably meeting in a scissors bite, though a level bite is permitted. Undershot mouths are greatly to be discouraged. It should be emphasized though, that a slightly undershot bite in an otherwise well-balanced head with correct sweet expression should not be penalized in favor of a level mouth with a plain head or hard expression.

Teeth: Strong and even, preferably meeting in a scissors bite, although a level bite is permitted. Undershot mouths are greatly to be discouraged; it should be emphasized however, that a slightly undershot bite in an otherwise well-balanced head with the correct sweet expression should not be penalized in favor of a level mouth with a plain or hard expression. Faults: Weak or crooked teeth, crooked jaws.

Correct:
Scissor bite

Incorrect:
Undershot bite

Incorrect:
Overshot bite

Discussion: The AKC Breed Standard for the Cavalier calls for a perfect scissors bite, while the Canadian and CKCSC, USA Standards permit a level bite, although a scissors bite is preferable. A level bite is when both upper and lower incisors touch. Some youngsters may exhibit a slightly undershot mouth up to as much as a year and a half of age. These puppies often have lovely heads with round, full muzzles and correct bites when they grow into adulthood. Teeth should be even and properly spaced. The jaw should be broad and full when viewed from the front.

Examples of correct breed type— male and female. Large round, dark eyes, gently rounded skull, full muzzle. Glamorous— complete with the blenheim spot.

IV. NECK, TOPLINE, AND BODY

Neck: Fairly long, without throatiness, well enough muscled to form a slight arch at the crest. Set smoothly into nicely sloping shoulders to give an elegant look.

Neck: Moderate length, without throatiness. Well enough muscled to form a slight arch at the crest. Set smoothly into nicely sloping shoulders.

Neck: Fairly long, without throatiness, well enough muscled to form a slight arch at the crest. Set smoothly into nicely sloping shoulders.

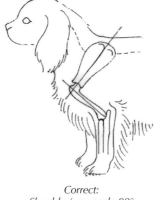

Correct:
Shoulder/arm angle 90°
Shoulder 45° to ground.

Incorrect:
Shoulder angle over 90°
Upright shoulder.

Discussion: A properly proportioned, arched neck flowing into well-angulated shoulders makes for a much more elegant picture than a neck that is too short, which creates a "stuffy" appearance. A properly set-on neck of the correct length will allow the dog to have elegant head carriage—a must in this breed. The lower line of the neck should not have a lot of dew lap underneath it but should flow tightly into the upper chest.

Topline: Level both when moving and standing.

Body: Short-coupled with ribs well sprung but not barreled. Chest moderately deep, extending to elbows allowing ample heart room. Slightly less body at the flank than at the last rib, but with no tucked-up appearance.

Body: Short-coupled with ribs well sprung but not barreled. Chest moderately deep leaving ample heart room. Back level. Slightly less body at the flank than at the last rib, but with no tucked up appearance.

Body: Short coupled with ribs well sprung but not barreled. Chest moderately deep, leaving ample heart room. Back level, leading into strong, muscular hindquarters. Slightly less body at the flank than at the rib, but with no tucked-up appearance.

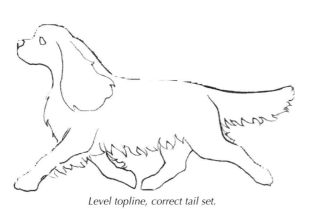

Level topline, correct tail set.

Dip in topline, tail carried too high.

Discussion: Short coupled means that the space between the ribs and the pelvis (called the loin) is not too long. Judges will often be seen measuring this by placing fingers against the loin, with three fingers being an average length. Bitches are allowed a slightly longer loin, to make room for puppies. The rib cage should be well rounded, allowing plenty of space for the heart and lungs. A barrel chest, on the other hand, is most unattractive and interferes with movement. A level back means just that. When viewed from the side, the back is level, without dip, roach, or slope from wither to tail.

Tail: Well set on, carried happily but never much above the level of the back, and in constant characteristic motion when the dog is in action. Docking is optional. If docked, no more than one third is to be removed.	*Tail:* Set so as to be carried level with the back. Tail should be in constant characteristic motion when the dog is in action. Docking is optional, but whether or not it is docked, the tail must balance the body, and the tails of broken-colored dogs should always be docked to leave a white tip.	*Tail:* Set so as to be carried level with the back. Tail should be in constant characteristic motion when the dog is in action. Docking is optional, but whether or not the tail is docked, it must balance the body. If docked, tail must not be cut too short. Two-thirds is the absolute minimum to be left on the body, and the tails of broken colored dogs should always be docked to leave a white tip.

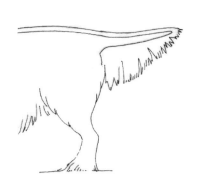

Correct tail set and carriage.

Incorrect. Gay tail.

Incorrect. Low, nervous tail set.

Discussion: Ideally, the tail should flow off of the dog's back in a straight line. It must not be carried up over the back in a circle, which is termed a "gay" tail, or down between the back legs, which is indicative of a poor temperament. Certain Cavaliers will exhibit dominant behavior by carrying their tails somewhat elevated, but this is not to be confused with a gay tail, which is a structural fault. Low tail sets and sloping croups are incorrect. Most importantly, the tail is a barometer of the dog's temperament and must be joyfully wagging at all times.

V. FOREQUARTERS

Shoulders well laid back. Forelegs straight and well under the dog with elbows close to the sides. Pasterns strong and feet compact with well-cushioned pads. Dewclaws may be removed.	*Forequarters:* Forelegs straight and well under the dog. Bone moderate. Elbows close to the sides. Shoulders should slope back with moderate angulation to give the characteristic look of top class and presence. Pasterns strong and feet compact, well feathered, and with well-cushioned pads.	*Legs:* Forelegs straight and well under the dog, bone moderate, elbows close to the sides.

Correct front.

Incorrect. Loose elbows, toeing-in.

Incorrect. Weak pasterns, toeing-out.

VI. HINDQUARTERS

The hindquarters construction should come down from a good broad pelvis, moderately muscled; stifles well turned and hocks well let down. The hind legs when viewed from the rear should parallel each other from hock to heel. Faults: Cow or sickle hocks.

Hindquarters: Hind legs moderately muscled, well angulated at the stifles. Hocks relatively short and at right angles to the ground when standing. Hind legs should parallel each other from hock to heel. The dog should stand level on all four feet.

Hind legs moderately muscled, stifles well-turned. Hocks well let down. The hind legs, viewed from the rear, should parallel each other from hock to heel. Pasterns strong and feet compact with well-cushioned pads. The dog stands level on all four feet. Faults: Loose elbows, crooked legs, stifles turned in or out, cow hocks, stilted action, weak pasterns, open feet.

Correct rear.

Incorrect. Cow-hocked

Incorrect. Hocks turning out - feet turning in.

Discussion: Moderate bone means bone that is neither too fine nor too heavy in proportion to the size of the individual. Cavaliers must not be coarse and common, neither must they exhibit the fragile or dainty characteristics of a Papillion. When viewed from above and standing correctly, the front feet of the dog should be in a straight line from the point of the shoulder blade to the toe. Elbows should be set closely to the body, with no tendency to elbowing out or pinching in the front. Pasterns should be almost straight—never badly sloping or weak. Back legs: Short hocks (well let down) are essential and must be perpendicular to the ground when viewed from the side or the rear. A dog with sickle hocks will move his legs with the motion of a scythe or sickle when viewed from the side, as the name implies. The dog will move without drive and will lack a ground-covering stride. A cow-hocked dog will stand with his hocks toward each other. Stifles should be moderately well bent (angulated), but not extreme. They should also be moderately muscled and broad when viewed from the side. The feet must not toe in or out in either front or rear. The descriptive term "tight feet" means that the foot is not open or splayed. Hind angulation should correspond with shoulder angulation; hence the term "balanced." A dog that is unevenly angulated in the front and rear—in other words, straight in front and overly angulated behind or vice versa—will not track properly.

The American Kennel Club

The Canadian Kennel Club

The Cavalier King Charles Spaniel Club, USA

VII. COAT

Of moderate length, silky, free from curl. Slight wave permissible. Feathering on ears, chest, legs and tail should be long, and the feathering on the feet is a feature of the breed.

Coat: Long, silky and free from curl, though a slight wave is permissible. Feathering on the ears, legs and tail should be long, and the feathering on the feet is a feature of the breed. No trimming, or artificial coloring of the dog is permitted. However, it is permissible, and often desirable, to remove the hair growing between the pads on the underside of the foot.

Coat: Long and silky and very soft to the touch, free from curl, though a slight wave is permissible. Feathering on ears, legs and tail should be long, and the feathering on the feet is a feature of the breed.

No trimming of the dog is permitted. Specimens where the coat has been altered by trimming, clipping, or by artificial means shall be so severely penalized as to be effectively eliminated from competition. Hair growing between the pads on the underside of the feet may be trimmed.

TRIMMING

No trimming of the dog is permitted. However, it is permissible and often desirable, to remove the hair growing between the pads on the underside of the foot.

Discussion: The coat is soft and silky and in healthy condition, has a luxurious sheen. While a slight wave is permitted, the coat must not be curly or unruly. The ears should be fully feathered, as should be the chest, the undercarriage, the legs and the tail. The feathering on the feet is a feature unique to the breed. Males will often carry more coat than bitches. On no account should the coat be hard or coarse. While the Cavalier should be exhibited in pristine and top condition, absolutely no artificial alteration of the coat by any means is allowed.

VIII. COLOR

1. Blenheim: Rich chestnut markings well broken up on a clear, pearly white ground. The ears must be chestnut, and the color evenly spaced on the head and surrounding both eyes, with a white blaze between the eyes and ears, in the center of which may be the lozenge or "Blenheim Spot". The lozenge is a unique and desirable, though not essential, characteristic of the Blenheim.

2. Tricolor: Jet black markings well broken up on a clear, pearly white ground. The ears must be black and the color evenly spaced on the head and surrounding both eyes, with a white blaze between the eyes. Rich tan markings over the eyes, on cheeks, inside ears and on underside of tail.

Blenheim: Bright chestnut red markings well broken up on a pearly white ground. The red on the head must extend around the eyes as well as down over the ears. There should be a white blaze between the eyes and ears in the center of which is the lozenge or "Blenheim Spot", unique within the Blenheim Cavalier King Charles Spaniel, a highly desirable, but not essential, characteristic of the Blenheim.

Tricolor: jet black markings well broken up on a pearly white ground. The black of the head must extend around the eyes as well as down over the ears. There should be a white blaze between the eyes. Rich tan markings appear over the eyes, on cheeks, inside ears, under tail and around the vent.

Blenheim: Rich chestnut markings well broken up on a pearly white ground. The ears must be red and the color evenly spaced on the head, with a wide white blaze between the ears, in the center of which is the much valued lozenge (diamond) or "Blenheim Spot". The lozenge is a unique and highly desirable, though not essential, characteristic of the Blenheim.

Tricolor: Jet black markings well broken up on a pearly white ground, with rich tan markings over the eyes, on cheeks, inside ears and on underside of tail.

The American Kennel Club	*The Canadian Kennel Club*	*The Cavalier King Charles Spaniel Club, USA*

3. Ruby: Whole: colored rich red.

4. Black and Tan: Jet black with rich tan markings over the eyes, on cheeks, inside ears, on chest, legs, and underside of tail.

Ruby: whole-colored rich red.

Black and Tan: jet black with rich tan markings over the eyes, on the sides of the muzzle, inside the ears, on the throat and chest, on the forelegs from the knees to the toes and on the hind legs on the inside of the legs, also extending from the hock to the toes, and on the underside of the tail and surrounding the vent.

Ruby: Whole-colored rich red.

Black and Tan: Jet black with rich tan markings over eyes, on cheeks, inside ears, on chest, legs and underside of tail.

Faults. White marks on whole-colored specimens, heavy ticking on Blenheims or Tricolors.

Blenheim	Tricolor	Ruby	Black & Tan

Discussion: The white on parti-colored Cavaliers has a distinctive pearly cast and must never be a dead or chalk white. Clown faces, i.e., white around only one or both eyes, are highly undesirable, because this distracts from the melting Cavalier expression. So important is this, it is considered a disqualification in the Canadian Kennel Club Standard. Markings on parti-colors should be well broken up. In a Blenheim, the markings should be rich, not lemon colored. Blenheims and tricolors must have a white blaze between the eyes. The chestnut markings should be rich and clearly defined with no tendency toward yellowing or sootiness. Rubies should be a rich red, not washed out or sandy looking. Furnishings are often lighter. Black and tans should be jet black, not rusted or brown, and the tan should be bright and clear, not smutty. While it is considered that white markings on whole colors and freckles on parti-colors are faults, to penalize an otherwise outstanding specimen for these cosmetic flaws is shortsighted. The degree of severity must be taken into consideration.

IX. GAIT

Free moving and elegant in action, with good reach in front and sound, driving rear action. When viewed from the side, the movement exhibits a good length of stride, and viewed from front and rear it is straight and true, resulting from straight-boned fronts and properly made and muscled hindquarters.

*Correct movement
Level topline.*

*Incorrect movement
Sway-backed, pacing.*

*Incorrect movement
Roached back.*

*Incorrect movement
Hackney.*

*Incorrect movement
Low head, nervous tail.*

The American Kennel Club

The Canadian Kennel Club

The Cavalier King Charles Spaniel Club, USA

X. TEMPERAMENT

Gay, friendly, non-aggressive with no tendency towards nervousness or shyness. Bad temper, shyness and meanness are not to be tolerated and are to be so severely penalized as to effectively remove the specimen from competition.

Temperament: Fearless and sporting in character, yet at the same time gentle and affectionate.

Disqualifications: Colors other than the four above. Clown faces (white around one eye or both or white ears). Undue aggressiveness, bad temper, snapping at judges.

It is important to remember that a dog can have one or more of the faults listed in the Standard, in moderation, and still be an overall typical, gay, elegant Cavalier. On the other hand, bad temper or meanness are not to be tolerated and shall be considered disqualifying faults. It is the typical gay temperament, combined with true elegance and "royal" appearance which are of paramount importance in the breed.

Discussion: Temperament is the single most important criteria of Cavalier breed type. Bad temper and meanness are disqualifying faults in the Canadian and CKCSC, USA Breed Standards, while the AKC Standard states "Bad temper, shyness, or meanness are not to be tolerated and to be so severely penalized as to effectively remove the specimen from competition." Cavaliers with the correct temperament are happy and outgoing showmen. A dog not exhibiting true Cavalier attitude and showmanship is not worthy of a ribbon.

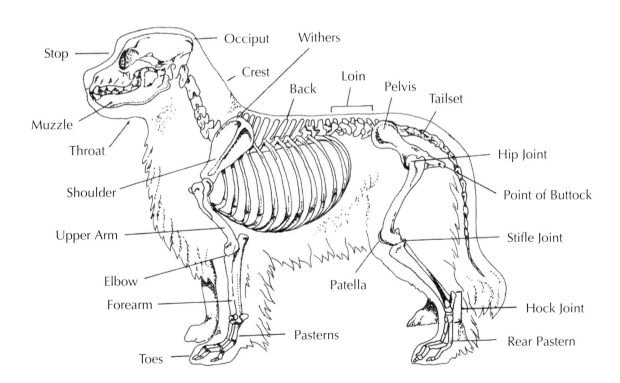

Elaine Mitchell with Cambridge Tommy Tu Tone and his son Canadian Champion Cambridge Flashdance.
This chapter on training was written under the direction of Elaine.

chapter eight

TRAINING THE CAVALIER PUPPY - *THE MITCHELL METHOD*

*D*reaming of the Blue Ribbon

At some point in your life as a Cavalier owner, your thoughts may turn to showing your dog. A vision flashes through your mind. Your little companion stands in front of you, gazing at you in rapt adoration, feet perfectly placed four-square and tail wagging gently. The judge walks down the line, and your dog shifts his gaze ever so slightly to the judge's face as if to demand the ribbon. The judge asks you to move again. Your little friend trots briskly along, head held proudly, tail wagging happily, a straight line out and back, never missing a step. He stops perfectly in front of the judge, and the audience sighs with pleasure. One more time

around and the judge points to you for first place, the breed, the Group, or even Best in Show.

A lovely picture, of course, but the reality is that your little friend that was so perfect in your mind may well turn into a little demon the minute you enter the show ring. When asked to look up, he immediately becomes fixated on some imaginary object between your feet. Examine his teeth on the table? Never! He turns to instant pudding! Ask him to walk a straight line—and he veers off to renew an old acquaintance at ringside. Then, horror of horrors, he regards the judge walking down the line

Thirteen year old Whitney Gee and Laughing Lady Castlemaine winning Reserve Winners bitch at the 1995 CKCSC, USA National Specialty under popular English breed specialist judge Pam Rooney. Photo by Meager.

as an entity from another planet and retreats between your legs! Needless to say, this sort of behavior will never win the coveted blue ribbon.

Getting the Puppy's Attention

Showing a Cavalier is somewhat like fly fishing or riding a horse; largely a question of mind over matter, but the fact that the "matter" has a mind of its own greatly contributes to the challenge. The single most important point in training of any kind is that you must have your Cavalier's attention at all times. When you have his attention, you must teach him what you want him to do, and you must be absolutely certain that he knows what you are asking when you give him a command. The biggest mistake that novice handlers make is to fail to notice that the dog does not fully understand the command that is being given. Then of course the puppy cannot fulfill the command—the owner mistakes this for disobedience and general confusion is the result—a no win situation for all involved. The novice frequently gives confusing directions, the result of which is a confused Cavalier. Confused dogs do one of two things—either they ignore what to them is senseless prattle and go merrily about their own business, or they become very submissive and frightened, and thus the puddle of pudding on the examining table. Always remember—in order for a dog to follow your instructions, he must first of all hear you, second understand your instructions and know how to comply, and thirdly he must be physically able to carry them out.

Training Sympathetically

Cavaliers are among the easiest of all breeds to train. Although they are not on the "top ten doggy intelligence" list, they are by nature very eager; in fact, they are anxious to please. They are easily motivated by food, praise, and enthusiasm. While they may be slower to learn than some, they are rarely bored by repetition and are not in the least cunning or devious. At the same time, they do not respond well to harsh training methods of any kind and often become confused or submissive when treated badly, leaving the less-than-patient trainer to conclude that they are either stupid or "wimps." Not at all. In the hands of a sympathetic trainer, they are a joy to show in both conformation and obedience competition.

Training with Behavior Modification

To train, I use a form of behavior modification that capitalizes on the Cavalier's attributes. While this chapter focuses primarily on training for show, this method is just as effective for obedience or for teaching the family friend. Even though your Cavalier may never enter the show ring, your veterinarian will be eternally grateful for a dog that stands patiently to be examined. A well-mannered dog is welcome nearly everywhere.

Let the Training Begin!

To ensure that you can get your Cavalier's attention whenever necessary, install an imaginary on-off switch right where the Blenheim spot should be. It is a well-known fact that Cavaliers are motivated by food, which means that food will be the power source for this switch. You also need an imaginary voice-activated remote control, so pick a word. Any short word will do, but trainers like words such as "yes!" because you can get them out quickly, and in public they can be reduced to a short hiss under the breath.

Ideally, you will start training the day you start weaning the puppy. Every time you set the food bowl down, say "yes!" Say it often and with enthusiasm so that your puppy will learn to greet this word with great excitement and will start running over to you whenever he hears it. When he does this, praise him lavishly and say the word again. The puppy comes to connect "yes!" with all good and positive things. In the beginning, the puppy is responding correctly by accident. It is your job to give plenty of positive reinforcement to the correct response—which is paying attention and coming over to you to see what you have for him whenever you say the magic word.

Whatever you do, do not pull or jerk on the puppy. Photo by Vavra.

Having his teeth checked is something every Cavalier must learn. Photo by Vavra.

Put the pupppy on a sturdy table with good footing and hold him securely. Photo by Vavra.

If you are starting with an older dog or a puppy that has not received this sort of preliminary training, the procedure will be the same but will take more time. Persevere—this is the gateway for all future training. For those of you who have older dogs that are not good eaters, take heart. There is not a Cavalier on this planet that will not beg from the table. Just use your magic word "yes!" with each tasty morsel, and before long you will have your dog's rapt attention each time you say the word. If you have two dogs or a litter of puppies, they will soon be competing for your attention. Say "yes!" and pop a goodie into their mouths, such as a tiny piece of hot dog or string cheese. Be fair, and be sure that everybody gets a treat. Always say "yes!" immediately before the treat. Some puppies will be a little more hesitant, so encourage them to come forward and reward them for being even a little more competitive. You want to bring out the best in each puppy. Once you have your puppy's attention, you have completed the most difficult hurdle of dog training. Everything else will be easy.

Training the Puppy to be Examined

At the same time that you begin attention training, you can also teach your puppy to be examined and to have his mouth looked at. To do this, turn him gently upside down in your lap, stroking him and talking to him gently until he relaxes. Some puppies accept this more willingly than others. Real squirmers must be held gently until the squirming subsides. Don't forget to say "yes!" over and over again and to give him plenty of treats. Rub his ears and handle his feet while he is on his back in your lap. The object of this exercise is to have the puppy relax and enjoy whatever you choose to do to him. Silly as it may sound, you will never have trouble cutting toenails if he has learned the "this little piggy went to market" nursery rhyme at nine weeks!

One of the things that Cavaliers resent most is having their mouths examined. With the puppy upside down in your lap, run a finger gently along the front of his gums. The puppy's head is supported by your knees so that he cannot learn to back off or to swing his head away from your finger. Again, gentle persistence is the key. A little butter on your finger makes this training infinitely more appealing. Cavalier mouths go through many changes, which drives breeders crazy, and it is tempting to wrench open a dog's mouth at every opportunity. Experienced breeders and judges can feel the set of the mouth with the forefinger without parting the lips. Having his teeth checked is something that every Cavalier must learn.

Once he is used to having his teeth felt, it is time to proceed to looking at them. Again, gentle persistence with a reward pays off, because Cavaliers are very mouth and head sensitive, particularly at teething time, and if you are rough or forceful, you could easily end up with a dog that is head shy for life.

Training the Puppy to Stand

Once your puppy is relaxed upside down in your lap and can be handled and examined without fuss, it is time to teach him to stand. Turn him right-side up, gently supporting him from the front with your right hand, by placing a couple of fingers between his front legs, and from the rear, by placing a couple of fingers from your left hand

The puppy must learn to stand four square, head up and back straight. B.J. The Alchemist at Hazelford, owned by Courtney Carter. Photo by Meager.

between his back legs. Gently put him on your knees with his front feet on your right leg and his back feet on your left leg. If he forgets his earlier training and resorts to wiggling, which he almost certainly will do, suspend him a couple of inches above your lap. Do not shake him, and resist the temptation to jounce him up and down, which accomplishes nothing. When he relaxes, set him down on your lap again. Here you can teach him a new word—"stand." Say it a million times, and do it a million times. Reward him with the magic word, followed immediately with food every time he stands even for the briefest of seconds.

You will notice that your puppy is starting to regard "yes!" as a treat as much as the actual goodie itself. This is great, because in obedience competition and in the conformation shows in some countries, it is against the rules to take food into the ring. In time, you will want to be able to give your Cavalier direction with or without having to offer food as a reward. Remember, however that Cavaliers are sometimes slow learners and are very food motivated. Being patient and taking slow steps are the key elements. If at any time during the training you find your puppy losing confidence,

acting overwhelmed, or balking at learning more, you are going too fast.

Always keep in mind that a Cavalier must be happy and wag his tail when he is working. He is never to be a wooden statue in the ring. Do not, particularly at a young age, emphasize perfect behavior over a happy disposition and a wagging tail. If you do, you will surely end up with an inanimate show dog. This is contrary to the Breed Standard's requirement for temperament and will not present a good picture to the public or contribute to your trophy collection.

Training to Stand on the Table

When your puppy is confident standing on your lap, you are ready to proceed to the table. Put the puppy on a sturdy table with good footing and hold him securely, just as you did when you placed him on your knees. Start from the beginning, and teach him again everything that he already knows, from lying upside down to standing on command. By going back over lessons that he has already learned, you are teaching the puppy to be relaxed and confident on the table. Now is a good time for the puppy to start wearing his own little buckle

Canadian Champion Turnworth Christina Wild, CD with owner/breeder Katie Eldred. Photo by Steven Ross.

collar—just so he can get used to the feel of it—and never as a restraint. He should only wear it under supervision or he might get it caught on something and come to harm.

Riding in the Car and Going to the Vet

You want your puppy's first two or three car rides to be happy experiences—around the corner to the drive-through ice-cream store for a "baby dish of vanilla, no spoon please" is appropriate. A couple of licks of ice cream will give your puppy some happy thoughts and not much to throw up! If he starts with short, pleasant trips at an early age, he will rarely feel the need to be car sick.

At the veterinarian's office, the puppy is again praised lavishly by you and the vet. An obliging veterinarian will give you time to relax the pup and will allow you to hold him while the shots are administered. The puppy will be more securely held this way, and there will be no traumatic table experiences. If the doctor wants to see the puppy's teeth, you can roll the puppy over in your arms and show off your well-behaved baby!

Training to Lead

To start lead training, you will need a handful of treats. Your puppy should be wearing his buckle collar, and you should take him to a secure area from which he cannot escape—preferably a quiet area or a room where he has never been before. There you are, alone with your puppy in a strange place with no distractions. You are his best friend, the giver of all good things, and you have the treats. What is the puppy going to do? Stick to you like glue, of course. Hold a fairly large piece of food right in front of his nose. He will follow that piece of food wherever your hand takes it. Give him a new word to think about, such as "walk." Let him follow your hand and the food, allowing him to take small bites as you go. A few sessions of this and your puppy will go with you wherever you go—and he is not even wearing his leash.

Your puppy is not trained at this point, he is only accidentally making the right moves most of the time. Your job is to reinforce the correct responses so that he will learn to do them all the time. A puppy is often erratic and unpredictable, and his attention span may be short. Do not take him out into an open, unsecured area without a lead, and never leave him unattended with his collar on. Do nothing that could endanger his life or health.

When the puppy will follow you willingly, it is time to snap a light lead onto his collar. Repeat the entire performance. Do not ever pull on the lead. If you do, the puppy will certainly pull back, and this is not what you want. Use food and your voice to get the appropriate response. Think of the lead as a cobweb that will break at the slightest tug. What you want to do is train the puppy to follow you whether or not he is wearing the lead. Your puppy must never learn that "on lead" is restriction and "off lead" is freedom. Rather, the puppy is bound to you by an invisible thread of enjoyment and trust.

Encouraging the Reluctant Puppy

Occasionally you will meet a puppy that will sit down and freeze, either in the first lessons without the lead or as soon as you snap on the lead.

Often this is a reserved puppy that does not have the confidence to get up and move around in a strange place. Do everything possible to encourage him to move. Reward even a step or two, because for a puppy that doesn't want to move, a single step is a big victory. Remember—he is not being willful or disobedient. He has no idea what you want. Whatever you do, do not pull or jerk on him, because this will cause him to become even more fearful. Sometimes working with a more outgoing littermate or a reliable older dog will encourage a reluctant puppy. A reliable older dog can be good encouragement/role model for a reluctant puppy too. Never push a puppy beyond his capabilities. Each puppy will be different and should be allowed to proceed at his own speed. The more outgoing puppy will catch on fast—so fast, in fact, that he may lose interest in you and the game that you are playing. If this happens, simply put him away. He will soon learn that if he loses interest in you, you will lose interest in him, and the fun ends.

Now you have a puppy that is almost lead trained, is relaxed and happy on a table, allows himself to be handled all over, and for the most part gives you his undivided attention.

Training the Puppy to Stack

The puppy's next lesson is stacking on the table. Being comfortable on the table is good, but

Socialization is a must at 12 weeks. Exposure to a variety of people and places is very important in developing a well-rounded, happy puppy. Photo by Vavra.

the puppy must now learn to stand four square, head up and back straight. Start by supporting his chin gently with your right hand. With your left hand, take his left front leg by the elbow and place it in position on the table. Gently move his head to the left to shift his weight and "anchor" that leg in place. Still holding his chin, take his right elbow and place his right leg parallel to the left one. Now gently move his head back and forth to balance his weight over both front legs. Tell the puppy that he is wonderful!

Now lift his left back leg by the hock and place it so that from heel to toe it is perpendicular to the ground. Use his head again to push his weight gently back onto that leg to anchor it. Take the right hock and place that leg parallel to the left one. Evenly distribute the puppy's weight by pushing his head gently in the appropriate direction.

At first he will only be able to hold a position for the briefest of moments, or you may only be able to place one or two legs before he moves. Gradually you can lengthen the time the puppy is required to stand. When he attempts to

Proper socialization will turn your puppy into a Cavalier that is a joy to be around. Laughing Maid by Magic, owned by Deborah Ayer. Photo by Victoria Plann.

move a foot, you can gently push his weight onto that leg, making it more difficult to move. Don't forget your command word "stand," plus "yes!" and lots of praise. Realize that the perfect show stance is only an idea at this stage. The puppy is just learning to be placed in a given position and to be still.

Meeting Strangers

When the puppy's vaccinations are complete, you can start taking him to public places to meet strangers. Pick someone who has a little dog knowledge and who will not frighten the puppy. Let him make all of the first advances. If he approaches the stranger, his new friend can reward him with "yes!" and a treat. On no account should the stranger force attention on the puppy, particularly on the more reserved puppy. In difficult cases, sit down with the puppy in your lap right next to the stranger. Carry on a normal

CKCSC, USA Champion Redthea Poppycock of Applegate. Record holding tricolor bitch for the CKCSC, USA. Owned by Karen Anderson. Photo by Meager.

conversation, and in time, curiosity will almost certainly overcome the youngster's hesitancy.

Once he is confident with a few different people and will accept food from them, you can start to introduce him to newcomers in a table situation. At first the puppy is not required to stand or perform on the table in any way, but merely to greet gift-bearing strangers with tail-wagging enthusiasm. When he has mastered this, he can graduate to walking up to strangers while on a lead on the floor.

Training to Bait

Now that the puppy will take food from your hand, it is a short step to teach him to bait. When you take him out by himself, feed him by hand. When he sits, as Cavaliers invariably do, just say "stand" and take a step toward him so that he is forced to move. The second he stands, beam "yes!" Reward him and keep repeating the command "stand" in a happy voice. It will not be long until he associates this word with the deed and the reward. As with all lessons, the reward must

immediately follow the action. Once he learns to stand and watch you, it is a simple maneuver to put the treat in his mouth and, still holding onto it, gently use it to pull the puppy into a position that pleases you.

Now your clever puppy has a rudimentary knowledge of everything that is required for ring success, and he is probably not even four months old!

Putting It All Together

You must work to put all of these separate elements into a ring-worthy performance. From now on, your puppy is not rewarded for every single attempt to oblige you. Treats and "yes!" do not come for merely loping along beside you anymore, but only when he trots a few steps. Soon he will figure out that trotting is what gets the reward. When he gets trotting down pat, you will reward for a specific speed. As the puppy becomes more and more accomplished, you reward for more specific behavior, and the puppy tries harder and harder to figure out exactly what you want.

Canadian and AKC Champion
Hilarny Larkin' About,
owned by Elaine Pinkowski.
Photo by Kurtis Photography.

Never chastise a puppy for making a mistake. He is not being disobedient — he is merely trying to figure out what you want. If you discipline him for guessing, he will stop trying to find out what pleases you and what brings him a reward. With each session, work more and more toward perfection, be it on the table or on the floor.

Puppies seem to learn so fast that there is a temptation to push them beyond their capabilities. Never be afraid to back up several steps in your training program, double both the "yes!" and the food reward as well as praise, and keep it fun. These steps take up mere moments of your time each day. They should be pleasurable for both you and your puppy. If not, stop and carry on when you both feel better.

Correcting the Puppy

Right in the middle of a good session, your now almost-perfect puppy may suddenly choose to ignore you. You know that he understands "yes!" because until now, the merest whisper of it has gained his whole attention. What will you do? It is time for the big "C" word. Correction! Correction is called for when a puppy ignores a command that he understands. Before you can correct a puppy, you must know that (a) the puppy has heard you, (b) he understands completely what you have asked him to do, and (c) he is physically able to comply. If these three criteria are fulfilled and he ignores the command, a correction is required.

And how do you correct a puppy? Exactly like his mother did—instantly, without any humor, and never, ever nagging. Once it is over, it is over. Pick a word that sounds unfriendly. "Uh uh!" "hey!" or "nah!" are all good ones. "No," however, lends itself to nagging. Keep a stern face. Think of the puppy's mother. She certainly has a serious look, even a snarl, for a serious offense. If the serious look and the word do not get his attention, add to this a simultaneous poke on the neck with your forefinger. I can guarantee that you will have the puppy's attention immediately. Ask for his attention again and the very instant you have it,

praise him lavishly and give him "yes!" After all, he has complied with your request for attention.

Never nag, because if you do, the puppy will learn that obeying or giving you his attention after he has been naughty is pointless, because you never let up. This sort of correction, incidentally, works for everything that you don't want the puppy to do, such as inappropriate barking, chewing, or digging in the lawn. The minute he stops doing what he is not to do and gives you his attention, you will reward him. Of course, it goes without saying that your puppy is never left unsupervised to learn bad habits. An untrained, unsupervised puppy soon learns what he can do when you are watching and what he can get away with when you are not there.

Attending Handling Classes

Once your puppy has a grasp of all of these exercises and is confident with strangers and in strange places, you may wish to attend a handling or socialization class. A word of caution: check out classes carefully before you commit yourself to them. You have raised your Cavalier puppy to this point with loving care and positive reinforcement. If you do not like the way your potential instructors treat their students, either human or animal, this is not the class for you. This is your puppy. Do not let anyone do anything that you feel will be detrimental to his well-being and happiness.

Look for classes that offer brief and varied sessions with lots of fun and positive reinforcement. Although boring, repetitive, military-style classes are almost a thing of the past, they are still out there and are to be avoided like the plague. Many classes are geared to teaching handling skills to the owner. These classes, while good, are not generally geared to the puppy's emotional advancement. What you are looking for is a socialization class for the puppy and a handling class for you. It is a rare and skilled instructor who can educate a puppy and novice owner at the same time to benefit both of you.

Relax and Enjoy

In all of the training, notice that every time you make something more difficult for the puppy, like asking him to meet people on the table rather than just being on the table without meeting people, you must make something else easier, like going back to asking only for the puppy to stay on the table rather than stack while he is meeting people. Then you can gradually build up his performance and confidence. Puppy training is not regimented. There are no hour-long formal training sessions. Puppy training is simply part of life's experiences. These simple exercises are indulgences that can be entered into for pure pleasure for both of you at any time during the day. They can take a few seconds or a few minutes—never more. Remember that you have a Cavalier for friendship and enjoyment. Show training and competing should enhance those aims. And when your puppy is clean and well trained, looking merrily up at you and wagging his tail as you enter the show ring, what is your job? *To relax and enjoy!*

At the end of a work session—relax and enjoy!

Exemplifying the true Cavalier personality—CKCSC, USA and Canadian Champion Laughing Stormin' Norman, owned by the author. Photo by Vavra.

CKCSC, USA and AKC Champion Ronnoc Celebration Time at Milestone, owned by Deborah Ayer and Constance Barton. Photo by Michael Allen

chapter nine
SHOWING YOUR CAVALIER

Showing at AKC, CKC, and CKCSC, USA Events

To exhibit in an AKC or CKC All Breed Show or Specialty, your Cavalier must be registered with the show giving organization, but you do not need to be a member of the breed club. Each organization has a set scale of points awarded per breed win, and to gain a championship title, a dog must attain a set number of points as well as a set number of majors. You can obtain this information from the parent club.

In CKC and AKC events, non-champion Cavaliers compete against each other for points and what are called "major" wins: Winners Bitch and Winners Dog. After the Winners Bitch and Winners Dog have been chosen those dogs that are already champions compete against Winners Bitch and Winners Dog for Best of Breed. After Best of Breed is awarded, Best of Winners will be awarded to either Winners Bitch or Winners Dog. Best of Opposite Sex is awarded to the best of the opposite sex to the Best of Breed winner. The Best of Breed Cavalier competes in the Toy Group, which has four placings. The dog that wins the group competes against all of the other group winners for Best in Show.

COMPARISON OF SHOW SYSTEMS

American Kennel Club	Canadian Kennel Club	Cavalier King Charles Spaniel Club, USA
• Dog must be registered with the AKC to exhibit. • Membership in parent club not necessary to exhibit. • Non-champions compete in the classes for Majors and points. • Champions, or "Specials" compete for BOB only. • Championship points required —15 points total, 2 major wins of three points or more.	• The dog must be registered with the CKC to exhibit. • Membership in parent club not necessary to exhibit. • If a US resident, the dog must have an events number. • Non-champions compete in the classes for points. • Champions, or "Specials" compete for BOB only. • Championship points required —10 pts, no major wins necessary.	• Dog must be registered with the CKCSC, USA . • Exhibitor must be a member in good standing of CKCSC, USA. • Champions and non-champions compete against each other for major wins and BIS. • 10 points, 2 major wins of three points or more.

Currently, for a championship title, the AKC requires fifteen points with two "majors" (a three-point win or better). The CKC requires ten points with no major wins necessary. The maximum points that can be won at any AKC or CKC show is five. Points awarded are dependent on the number of dogs exhibited. The point scales change from time to time, so it is best to check with the AKC or CKC for the current point ratings in your area.

In the CKCSC, USA, champions may compete against non-champions in the classes, making championship titles harder to attain. All undefeated dogs compete for Winners Dog, and all undefeated bitches compete for Winners Bitch. Winners Bitch competes against Winners Dog for Best in Show, Reserve Best in Show and Best of Opposite Sex.

Professional handlers are not permitted other than to exhibit dogs in their ownership. To exhibit in CKCSC, USA events, your Cavalier must be registered with and you must be a member in good standing of the club.

For a CKCSC, USA Championship title, a Cavalier must accumulate ten points at a CKCSC, USA Championship show. These ten points must include two major wins of three points or better, under two different judges in two different shows, in addition to at least one point under a third judge.

The time spent in training your Cavalier, will be well worth the effort when you start working as a team.

Canadian Champion Sanickro Strands of Gold with handler Jean Tremblay and Judge Virginia Lyne.
Photo by Alex Smith Photography.

Grooming equipment. Photo by Vavra

Preparing for the Ring

When you have trained your puppy, it is time to turn your attention to preparing yourself. If you have never shown before, attend handling classes. Among other things, you must learn the required patterns—a circle, a triangle, a diagonal, and occasionally a tee. If you are a novice, you can practice these figures without the dog. You may feel silly at first, but once you can get through the routine without thinking, it will be much easier to do it with the dog. If possible, take an older dog to class or borrow a retired show dog. You can learn many valuable lessons from a wise old campaigner and your future star won't become bored. Go to shows and watch the top handlers, because each has his own particular style and way in which he will show off his dog's virtues and hide his faults.

Cavaliers are a natural breed and should be shown accordingly. They should be shown on a loose lead, at a natural pace, neither galloped around the ring nor moved too slowly. They should be baited into position rather than being stacked by

hand on the floor. At no time should a handler be on their kness stacking a Cavalier. The Cavalier's naturally happy disposition should not be suppressed; in other words, the dog should be animated and alert, not a robot. Showmanship gives the judge a good indication of the Cavalier's temperament, which should be manifested through the characteristic, happy wagging of the tail.

Crowding has no place in the show ring. Not only will you annoy the person in front of you, but if the person behind gets too close, you will be trapped with no room to show off your exhibit. Space yourself, being ever watchful as to where the judge is looking. When you have your Cavalier set up, be aware of how the dog looks from the judge's point of view. Pick a flattering angle that will show off your dog's best features. Never stop showing your dog until the last ribbon is handed out, because you never know when a judge is going to unexpectedly turn around and look. Make your point, but be subtle. Over-handling, fidgeting, and constantly waving the bait in front of the dog's nose detracts from the overall picture.

CKCSC, USA and AKC Champion
Ravenrush Best Dressed of Luxxar,
owned by Paula Campanozzi. Photo by Meager.

Show Grooming

The Cavalier King Charles Spaniel must be flawlessly turned out when entering the show ring. The Breed Standard calls for no trimming, but there is no excuse to exhibit a dog that is poorly kept, in bad condition, and anything but spotlessly clean.

Beauty begins from within. If your dog is not in the peak of good health and free from internal and external parasites, this will certainly reflect in his outward appearance. Conditioning begins many months before a show and starts with a complete health check. A good diet, along with plenty of fresh air and exercise, is critical. Different dogs will do best on different types of food, and sometimes experimentation is necessary. Supplements that enhance hair growth may be added to the food, such as a teaspoon of corn oil added daily. Although a Cavalier's coat is his crowning glory, physical condition is also absolutely essential. A dog that is out of condition will not only move poorly, he will not have the stamina to stand up to vigorous campaigning. Nails must be trimmed regularly, because failing to do so can cause the dog to walk on his pastern instead of his toes, and therefore to move improperly.

Keeping your Cavalier Clean

A show dog's hair is gold and must be treated as such. Some Cavaliers are genetically predisposed to grow more hair, while others are not quite so well endowed. It is your job to preserve what they do grow. Dirt is the greatest enemy of the hair coat. In fact, the undercoat will be ripped out and the ends annihilated, if it is brushed when dirty—a sure way to never have the length of furnishings desired.

Removing Tangles

Before working on the coat, mist very slightly with a very dilute coat conditioner. Check for mats and tangles. These must never be ripped out with a slicker brush or comb, but spritzed with

CKCSC, USA Champion Wyndcrest Apollo.
Owned and bred by Mr. and Mrs. Harold Letterly.
Photo by Digital Artisry.

a detangler, then teased out carefully with the fingers and a pin brush. Forget that there is such a thing as a mat slicer. Every hair that is pulled out or that is left behind in the brush is not on the Cavalier that you want to be showing. It may take a long time, but it is well worth any effort spent. Ideally, never allow tangles to happen in the first place—but this is rather unrealistic! Cavaliers are a shedding breed however, and when they begin to shed it is best to bite the bullet and get the dead hair out as soon as possible, allowing for the new growth.

Choosing Shampoos

If your Cavalier is a parti-color and has stained feet and furnishings, there are stain removing and whitening shampoos on the market. There are also products that can be applied to the coat without water, called waterless shampoos, but these can be drying to the coat and can roughen up the hair cuticle, making it stain even more easily the next time. For this reason, it is of paramount importance to try to keep your Cavalier clean and stain-free at all times throughout his show career. An ounce of prevention is worth an ounce of cure, as it is nearly impossible to take a dog that is stained and give him the pearly white called for in the Standard. Antacids can reverse the acidity of a dog's system to avoid stains caused by drooling and licking. Bleach has no place on a Cavalier's coat. It makes the hair fragile and breakable and also opens up the hair shaft, leading to even more serious staining. Your veterinarian or equipment supplier may be able to help you, but booths at dog shows carry a wide variety of supplies geared specifically to show dogs, and these booths are generally staffed by knowledgeable people. Anything that is labeled for setter-type coats will work for the Cavalier.

Bathing and Drying

Bathe your Cavalier as described in the general grooming section and towel off the excess water. From here there are two methods: either blow dry the hair completely, or if your Cavalier

It is of paramount importance to try to keep your Cavalier clean and stain-free at all times throughout his show career. Canadian Champion Mingchen Rockafella. #1 Cavalier in Canada—1995 and 1996. Owned by June and Gerald Knobel. Photo by Janine Starink.

has some wave to the coat, the body can be toweled down to dry while the fringes are blown dry. To towel down, you need a towel that is slightly longer than the Cavalier, and four or five diaper pins. Spread the towel out, and fold the top one-third back. Turn the towel over, keeping the fold intact, then roll it up from the opposite end of the fold, gathering the folded piece as you go. Place your Cavalier in show position, and with your slicker brush, brush the body coat flat and in the direction the hair grows. You may at this point use a slight misting of setting lotion. Holding the towel tightly right behind the ears, pin the towel firmly underneath the ears, right under the chin. Keeping the hair flat, unroll the towel and pin again at the breastbone. Unroll the towel a bit more and pin underneath the chest behind the elbows. Unroll the towel some more, keeping the hair flat, and pin underneath the flank. Be particularly careful when you are pinning a male! Continue to unroll the towel and pin it under the tail.

Now proceed to blow dry the ears. Sit the Cavalier on a table in front of you and, with the blow dryer on low heat, brush and dry the ears at the same time using a pin brush. It is important to aim the air at the base of the hair and not at the ends, as this causes breakage. Blow and brush in the direction you want the hair to lie. Proceed until the ear is completely dry, then do ear number two.

At this point, if your dog is not pinned in a towel, proceed to dry the chest. Brush and blow the hair up toward the chin to give it fullness. Then, with your slicker brush, blowing and brushing in the direction you want the hair to lie, start at the back of the head, and dry the neck and body hair, working toward the tail. You can dry the front leg furnishings straight back so that the dog won't appear out at the elbows.

Next, stand your Cavalier, finish the body and continue brushing the pants and tail furnishings straight down. Make sure that you dry the hock hair up and brush the toe furnishings toward the center so that the dog won't appear to toe out, either in the front or rear.

It is absolutely essential that your Cavalier be completely dry, because if you put him away damp, he could catch a chill or iron his hair into the direction on which he happens to be lying. If your Cavalier is toweled, you may put him in a crate after you have dried the ears and other exposed furnishings. Allow him to dry completely with a warm dryer blowing into the crate. Never, ever leave a dog unattended in a closed crate with a dryer or when toweled, because he could become overheated or get tangled in his towel. When a toweled Cavalier is unwrapped, you may have to redampen and blow some of the furnishings straight.

Invariably, between bath and show, body coats will become curly, furnishings will become soiled, and ears will become kinky. When you reach the show, it is advisable to mist your dog's body coat down lightly, brush it into place, and re-towel. Your Cavalier can then go away to have a rest until he is dry. After exercising him before ring time, you may wish to wash the ears and furnishings with one of the waterless shampoos. Although they say "rinseless," these shampoos do build up, so rinse the ears and furnishings in a bowl of warm water after each application. Spray lightly with a diluted leave-in conditioner and proceed to blow dry as described previously. Your exhibit is ready to step into the ring.

Are you?

SHOW EQUIPMENT CHECK LIST

- Show lead and regular walking lead
- Grooming equipment
- Crate
- Exercise pen and paper (optional)
- Grooming table
- Dryer and extension cord
- Towels and pins
- Food and water bowls
- Home or bottled water
- Bait
- Entry conformation and directions to show
- Poop scoop and clean-up bags
- Show clothes for yourself
- Portable chairs
- Health and rabies certificate if applicable
- Shade tarp for summer
- Dog

Grooming the Exhibitor

Proper ring attire consists of neat, clean, appropriate clothing—with a pocket for bait. In North America, it is considered poor taste to wear jeans, jogging suits, or the like in the show ring. Men usually wear suits and ties, women dresses, skirts or dressy slacks. If you don't have a pocket for bait, a small but inconspicuous bait bag is permissible. In short, dress conservatively and in good taste. You want all attention to be focused on your exhibit.

Canadian Champion Halfmoon Shortbred Cookie, CD, with owner Phyllis Shortt and Judge Pam Thornhill of Kindrum Cavaliers, England. Shown winning Best of Opposite Sex at the 1993 Canadian National Specialty. Photo by Meager.

Dress conservatively and in good taste. CKCSC, USA and AKC Champion Partridge Wood Laughing Misdemeanour with owner/handler Cindy Lazzeroni. Shown winning a Group Four at the 1997 Westminster Kennel Club show. Photo by Ashbey Photography.

Breed type is what makes a breed uniquely itself. Elegant black and tans. Photo by David Dalton.

chapter ten
PLANNING TO BREED

A reputable breeder has improvement of the breed as his goal and is willing to do all that is necessary to ensure that any puppies produced by him are mentally and physically sound. Before breeding, a thorough study of the Breed Standard should be made, as even though the Standard is quite specific, it is open to interpretation. Attend as many shows as possible to develop an eye for correct type, and talk to different breeders about individual bloodlines—their strengths and their weaknesses. When you are learning to evaluate Cavaliers, it is important to look at the best, because comparisons between mediocre or indifferent dogs teaches little. Only by looking at quality will you develop an eye for quality. Start slowly with the best Cavalier that you can acquire, then begin exhibiting The reason a dog wins or loses will teach you which virtues are to be rewarded, which faults are likely to be judged harshly and which are more likely to be forgiven.

Breeding to the Standard

Responsible breeders want to know that their puppies will grow up to meet the Standard. To accomplish this, both sire and dam must be healthy, sound and of excellent breed type. Breed type is what makes a breed uniquely itself, and is the sum total of characteristics called for in the Breed Standard. Soundness is correct bone structure as

CKCSC, USA Champion Saintbrides Sail-On-Sailor, owned by Pam Burkley with his young son, CKCSC, USA Champion Falling Springs Helmsman, owned by Barbara Grimm Curley. Photo by Halgwood.

well as correct movement. Cavaliers should be "fearless and sporting in character, yet at the same time gentle and affectionate." While everyone wants a Cavalier to have the physical attributes that make this breed so alluring, health and disposition must be considered above all. Every Cavalier born should have the innate chance of a healthy life, and the only way to achieve this is to breed from Cavaliers that are of a mentally and physically sound family back-ground. The fact that an inferior Cavalier may win in the show ring does not mean that he should be used for breeding.

Linebreeding, Inbreeding, and Outcrossing

Linebreeding is the breeding of two animals that are not of the same parentage but who share common, although not closely, related ancestors. It is generally accepted that linebreeding is the best way to achieve and maintain desirable qualities. By using dogs of a common but not closely related ancestry, the gene pool is smaller; therefore, certain traits are more likely to breed true.

Inbreeding is the breeding of two closely related animals; for example, mother to son, father to daughter, and the closest of all breedings, brother to sister. This is not an advisable practice except by the most experienced breeders, because although desirable qualities can result, so can weaknesses, deformities, and poor temperament. Inbreeding is a quick way to reveal the genetic strengths and weaknesses of a line, but it must be undertaken with the knowledge that while the consequences can be outstanding, they also can be disastrous.

Outcrossing is the breeding of two unrelated animals, or animals whose common ancestors are so far back in the pedigree that they have little influence. Outcrossing is useful when it is necessary to increase the size of the gene pool. It is also a method used to introduce positive traits

lacking in an established line, although negative traits may be just as easily introduced. It must be realized that while undesirable recessive genes may be suppressed by outcrossing, they are not eliminated and may appear in subsequent generations.

Calculating Percentages

To calculate the influence of a particular dog in a proposed breeding, use the following chart. Great champions are not necessarily great producers, so concentrate on individuals that are known to produce well. Using a red pencil, circle the names of these dogs each time they appear in a pedigree, then assign the percentage of influence to each occurrence, and simply add them up. By doing this, you should be able to get some idea of their influence.

PEDIGREE PERCENTAGES	
Sire or dam	50% of the pedigree
Grandsire or granddam	25% of the pedigree
Great grandparent	12.5% of the pedigree
Ancestor in the 5th generation	6.25% of the pedigree
Ancestor in the 6th generation	3.13% of the pedigree
Ancestor in the 7th generation	1.56% of the pedigree
Ancestor in the 8th generation	.78% of the pedigree

Genetics

All of the instructions that determine whether a fertilized egg will develop into a rhinoceros, for instance, or a Cavalier King Charles Spaniel, are coded as combinations of four amino acids along a very long, helical molecule called DNA. Just as a magnetic tape holding a computer program travels past a head that reads the code and tells the computer what to do, living cells contain molecular structures that travel along a strand of DNA. These molecular structures read the pattern of amino acids and direct the manufacture of all the chemical substances that will generate the cells characteristic of a particular animal or plant. The section of code that governs a given characteristic is called a gene. In order that offspring are not exact copies of their parents, which would make evolution impossible (too slow to permit adaptation to changing environments, in any case), genes always exist in pairs, one-half of each pair being contributed by each parent, shuffled and combined at random at the moment of fertilization.

Dominant and Recessive Genes

Each gene of a pair is either dominant or recessive, which is to say that in a gene pair consisting of a dominant gene from one parent and a recessive one from the other, the dominant gene rules. Recessive genes are only expressed (have an effect on the developing organism) when they are inherited as both members of a gene pair, in which case they are said to be "reinforced."

In general, the dominant genes are those that best favor survival in the wild. The difference between the Cavalier and his wolf-like ancestor is due to the gradual elimination of many dominant wolfish genes. This process, desirable as it might be, is not without its dangers. Some recessive genes are highly undesirable, although some, like Blenheim coloration are highly desirable. In the process of reinforcing desired recessives, it is all too easy to reinforce others conferring health or temperament problems at the same time. The more highly inbred the animal, the more likely this is to occur. Once this happens in a breed, the only cure is outcrossing.

Understanding Dominant and Recessive Genes

To see how dominant-recessive genes work, let us look at the case of a simple, hypothetical breed whose coat is either pure white or pure black, the color being determined by a single gene pair, and black being dominant. We can label these genes B and w, the capital letter signifying a dominant gene.

A black animal is either pure black, having the gene pair BB; or hybrid black, having the pair Bw. The only way it can be white is if it carries a pair of reinforced recessive white genes, ww. Upon mating, the gene combinations are shuffled, so that in the case of a pure black mated with a

Four generations of Joan and Oliver Twigg's Culloden Cavaliers. Left to Right: Culloden Xandra, Culloden Margaret, Culloden Full of Grace and CKCSC, USA Champion Tuesday's Child of Culloden. Photo by Twigg.

(necessarily) pure white, all the resulting puppies will be hybrid black. Symbolically:

	B	B
w	Bw	Bw
w	Bw	Bw

There is no way of telling by looking at these black puppies whether they are pure or hybrid. The only way to find out for sure is to let them grow up and mate them with a white. Then, if the resulting litter contains any white puppies at all, you would know that your black dog was a hybrid, because:

	B	w
w	Bw	ww
w	Bw	ww

The lesson in general is that if you want to know if your dog carries a given recessive gene, mate him to one that you know does, and see if that gene is expressed in any of the puppies. While this is fine for a benign characteristic like coat color, we would emphatically not recommend this procedure to find the recessive gene for a defect like PRA.

The Real World of Color Genetics

In the preceding paragraphs, in order to illustrate the principle, we looked at a very simple, fictitious breed in which one gene pair controlled coat color. Among real dogs, things are a lot more complicated. No less than six gene pairs are involved, labeled conventionally A, B, C, D, E, and S. And they can all be either dominant or recessive, the dominant form conferring the characteristic and the recessive suppressing it. Because of their highly bred nature, all Cavaliers have the same A, B, C, and D genes, so we only have the two, E and

S, to worry about. The picture is still a little more complicated than our fictitious example.

The gene pair E (dominant) and e (recessive) controls whether there is black in the coat, while the pair S (dominant) and s (recessive) controls whether the coat is of a solid color or broken with white.

Genetic Makeup of the Blenheim

The genetic makeup of a Blenheim is therefore easy. Since there is no black in the coat, the recessive e must have been reinforced, suppressing it. And the coat is broken with white so that the recessive s gene must have been reinforced, suppressing a solid color. The Blenheim's makeup must therefore be ee:ss. This explains the well-known breeder's rule of thumb that breeding Blenheims to Blenheims always yields Blenheims. It could not do anything else, because there are no dominant genes to interfere.

Harana Courtney, owned by Kathy Gentil.
Photo by Digital Artistry.

Genetic Makeup of the Ruby

Rubies are not much harder. As before, there is no black, but this time there is a solid color. Thus, the ruby has to be either ee:SS or ee:sS. It is worth noting that in the latter case, although S is dominant, the presence of s often results in mismarking, or odd patches of white. If both ruby parents carry the recessive s gene, Blenheims will probably appear in the litter as well.

Genetic Makeup of the Tricolor

A tricolor carries the black E gene, either pure or hybrid, and because it does not have a solid coat color, must carry s reinforced. Its genotype, then, is either EE:ss or Ee:ss. Breeding tricolors to each other results in tricolor puppies, unless both parents are Ee:ss, in which case there may be tricolors and Blenheims in the litter.

Genetic Makeup of the Black and Tan

The black and tan is the most complicated genotype, because it carries dominant genes for both blackness and solid (no white) color. There are four possibilities that can add up to a black and tan: EE:SS, Ee:SS, EE:Ss and Ee:Ss. Only if both black and tan parents are EE:SS will they breed true.

Multiplying out the Possibilities

Once the genotypes of both parents are known, figuring out what is going to happen in any given mating is simply a matter of multiplying out the possibilities. Take for example the maximally complicated case of crossing two black and tans, each having the genotype Ee:Ss. You will get:

EE:SS	black and tan
Ee:SS	black and tan
Ee:Ss	black and tan
ee:SS	ruby
ee:Ss	ruby, possibly with white markings
EE:ss	tricolor
ee:ss	Blenheim

You will not necessarily get all of these combinations in one litter; however, these are the possibilities obtained by multiplying out the cross. The result, statistically, of a large number of such crosses would be one-ninth Blenheim, two-ninths ruby, two-ninths tricolor, and four-ninths black and tan.

Using the Knowledge

In order to use this knowledge, you must somehow figure out the genotypes of each member of the breeding stock or, more precisely, which recessive genes each carries. With careful reference to the pedigree and offspring, this can usually be determined following these rules:

Blenheims:	Are easy — always ee:ss
Rubies:	If a Ruby has produced any puppies at all that are either Blenheim or tricolor, then his genotype is ee:Ss. Otherwise he is probably EE:SS, but check his ancestry to be sure.
Tricolors:	If a tricolor has produced any puppies at all that are ruby or Blenheim, his genotype must be Ee:Ss. Otherwise it is probably EE:ss, but check his ancestry to be sure.
Black and tans:	The combinations are too complicated to be of much value.

Colors Bred	**Resulting Puppies**
Blenheim to Blenheim	All Blenheims
Blenheim to tricolor	Some Blenheims, some tricolors, sometimes all of one color or the other. In the case of all tricolors, the tricolor parent will usually be of a predominantly tricolor background.
Tricolor to tricolor	Usually all tricolors, frequently without good tan markings and heavily marked. If the tricolor parents have Blenheim in their backgrounds, the litter may include Blenheims.
Black and tan bred to black and tan	All black and tan, unless both parents have parti-color backgrounds, then all four colors can result.
Ruby to ruby	All ruby, same as above
Black and tan to ruby	Some black and tan, some ruby. In the case of all black and tans, the black and tan parent will usually be of a predominantly black and tan background.
Black and tan or ruby to tricolor or Blenheim	All four colors if both parents carry particolor genes. If the black and tan parent carries only whole color genes, all puppies will be black and tan. Most commonly, mis-marked black and tans and rubys (white markings). Occasionally no mis-marks.

Consistency in the above two litters of Pinecrest Cavaliers. Photo by Eubank.

Breeding for similarity of type. Chadwick Cavaliers. Photo by Anne Robins.

Polygenetic Inheritance

Some characteristics, such as the richness of coat color, the darkness of the eye, and hip dysplasia, are not governed by simple pairs of genes, but by a number of genes acting in concert. The more polygenes expressed, the stronger the characteristic, which is why the color red, for instance, and hip dysplasia are not either present or absent, but exist in varying levels. Polygenes, like the genes discussed above, exist in both dominant and recessive forms, richness of coat color being dominant and hip dysplasia being recessive. Genes can also carry modifiers, which cause the same gene to be expressed somewhat differently in animals which carry identical combinations of genes.

Among Cavaliers, there are probably no individuals entirely free of, for example, hip dysplasia polygenes, but among good breeding stock, these will be few enough that those (recessive) genes that are reinforced are insufficient to cause the abnormality. Fortunately, there is a threshold effect that works with the polygenes for most abnormalities such that it takes a certain minimum number of them expressed for the characteristic to manifest itself at all.

While the threshold effect is good for dog breeders, it is a nightmare for geneticists because, combined with the number of (probably not identical) genes needed to cause a given characteristic, it makes it very nearly impossible to work out the genetics of polygenes. For this reason, comparatively little is known about them, and what is known is not very useful. When it comes to characteristics governed by polygenes, even with the best of modern knowledge, you can do little more than breed the healthy to the healthy and hope for the best.

Canadian and CKCSC, USA Champion Salador Codogan of Honeycott, owned by William and Gerry Sloan. Photo by Wm. Sloan.

Inherited Health Disorders

The fact that there are inherited health problems in any breed does not mean that all dogs are affected. Reputable breeders are particularly vigilant to guard against severe disorders which are known to be hereditary. It should be kept in mind that the existence of disease, carried by recessive genes, means that two perfectly healthy parents may still produce affected offspring.

Two important terms to differentiate are congenital and hereditary. Congentital means "born with" (although not necessarily apparent at birth) may be genetic or acquired. Hereditary means genetically transmitted only—may or may not be present at birth.

All Cavaliers that are going to be used for breeding should have basic health clearances. The four clearances recommended are OFA or Penn Hip hip certification, CERF eye clearance, vet acknowledgment of normal patellas, and a normal heart, preferably verified by a veterinary cardiologist. OFA clearance does not need to be repeated; CERF, patella and heart testing should be done annually.

Heart Disease

Mitral Valve Disease (MVD) is of such concern that all Cavaliers should have their hearts checked before they are bred from, as well as given annual check-ups throughout their breeding careers. Until some definitive information is available, the only hope of reducing the incidence

AKC and Canadian Champion Happy Boy of Fairtale Forest. Owned by Dr. Morag Gilchrist. Photo by Nancy.

*The desire to create the perfect dog is the
goal of most breeders.
Photo by Eubank.*

of MVD is through careful breeding practices. A recent study done in Sweden showed that many Cavaliers develop a heart murmur by six or seven years old, and by eleven years old 100% have a heart murmur. The conclusion of the Swedish study was that Cavaliers used for breeding should be at least 2 1/2 years old and free from MVD, and their parents should be at least 5 years old and free from MVD. This should lessen the chance of their offspring being affected at a young age quite considerably.

Drs. Buchanan and Beardeau of the University of Pennsylvania have been conducting a study of the Cavalier King Charles Spaniel and mitral valve disease for a number of years, and the Cavalier King Charles Spaniel Club of Canada has also been involved in a similar study at the University of Guelph, under the direction of Dr. Michael O'Grady. As heart studies progress, up-to-date information will be made available through the breed clubs. It is important that breeders be guided by veterinary experts in the field, and not follow trends set forth by non-professionals. Check with breed clubs for information regarding seminars, publications and continuing research.

Patellar Luxation

Patellar luxation is not always inherited; it can also be due to stretching the tendon from injury. Patellar Luxation has a polygenic mode of inheritance. Dogs and bitches affected with hereditary patellar luxation should not be used for breeding.

Hip Dysplasia

E.A. Corley, executive director of the Orthopedic Foundation of Animals, (OFA) writes:

Canine hip dysplasia (CHD) is generally accepted to have a polygenic mode of inheritance. That is, the disease is due to the interaction of multiple genes with the environment. How many genes are involved is unknown but some scientists speculate the number of involved genes to be three or four. It is important to note that no environmental factor/s have been shown to cause CHD; however, environmental factors, i.e.: nutrition etc., may hide or exacerbate the radiographic changes of CHD in the genetically dysplastic dog."

From January 1974 to December 1995, 857 Cavaliers had their hip X-rays submitted to OFA, 10 percent of which were diagnosed as dysplastic. A case could be made that Cavaliers have only a 10 percent incidence of hip dysplasia; on the other hand, with such a small number of radiographs being submitted in this twenty-one-year period, it could be said that not nearly enough X-rays were analyzed to arrive at an accurate figure.

Hip X-rays can be sent to the OFA when a dog is less than two years old for a preliminary report, but a rating and permanent number are not assigned until the dog is X-rayed after his second birthday.

OFA uses the following method of classifying hip dysplasia:

- Excellent Conformation
- Good Conformation
- Fair Conformation
- Borderline Conformation/ Intermediate
- Mild degree of dysplasia
- Moderate degree of dysplasia
- Severe degree of dysplasia

The latest method of diagnosing hip dysplasia is Penn Hip, where the dog is positioned and X-rayed so that the "passive hip laxity" can be measured. The advantage of the Penn Hip evaluation over OFA is that hips can be X-rayed and an accurate diagnosis made as young as sixteen weeks of age. It is worth noting that, probably due to their small size, dysplastic Cavaliers do not necessarily become lame.

Eye Diseases

Although the percentage of Cavaliers suffering from blinding eye disease is relatively small, this does not mean that Cavaliers used for breeding should not have their eyes checked annually by a veterinary opthalmologist.

Cataracts

Cataracts can be inherited but are most frequently acquired. The most commonly inherited variety are juvenile cataracts. The acquired variety can be senile (old-age) cataracts, diabetic, nutritional, or from injury. Cataracts can be surgically removed, but if left untreated, other complications, such as glaucoma can result. Those with inherited cataracts should not be used for breeding.

Progressive Retinal Atrophy

Uncommon in Cavaliers, progressive retinal atrophy (PRA) is an incurable, inherited disease of the retina that causes blindness. No affected Cavaliers, or known carriers of the disease should be used for breeding. Both the parents and most of the offspring of a dog with PRA are carriers and should not be used for breeding.

Corneal Lipidosis

Corneal lipidosis or Lipid Keratitis is quite prevalent in Cavaliers. These corneal deposits are often caused by a low thyroid condition or high blood levels of cholesterol and triglycerides. Frequently appearing in first one eye and then the other, the opacities customarily resemble a doughnut in shape. The eye is often inflamed, which can be temporarily alleviated by administering drops obtained from a veterinarian. The deposits usually disappear within a year or two and do not interfere with vision. Check thyroid, cholesterol, and triglyceride levels and feed your Cavalier a low-fat diet. A dog with Corneal Lipidosis is not usually prohibited from breeding.

Retinal Dysplasia

Retinal dysplasia, which is being seen more frequently in Cavaliers, is a congenital malformation of the retina. According to the Canine Eye Registration Foundation (C. E. R. F.), retinal dysplasia has three forms: retinal folds, which are folds in the retina itself; geographic, an irregularly shaped area of development; and retinal detachment, which is a detachment of the retina itself. Geographic and detached retinal dysplasia are associated with blindness, and Cavaliers affected with either of these forms of retinal dysplasia should not be used for breeding.

Entropion and Distichiasis

Excessive tearing can be caused by entropion, the inward rolling of the upper eyelid, or distichiasis, which are abnormally located eyelashes that irritate the cornea. Both conditions can be surgically corrected.

Freedom!
Healthy, happy and enjoying life. One of the many generations of Laughing Cavaliers. Photo by the author.

Regis Chelsie of Pinecrest, CKCSC, USA & AKC Ch. Pinecrest Santa's Pleasure, CKCSC, USA & AKC Ch. Ravenrush Tailor Made of Pinecrest and Canadian & AKC Ch. Pinecrest Sweeney Todd. Owned by Mary Grace and Ted Eubank. Photo by Eubank.

chapter eleven
MATING AND WHELPING

The Stud Dog

A popular male that stands at public stud can have a significant impact on the breed due to the tremendous number of bitches that it is possible for him to breed. A good bitch, on the other hand, is limited to the number of litters that she can produce in her lifetime, so obviously her impact is reduced by comparison. A stud dog must therefore be sound physically and mentally and, of course, be of excellent breed type, without compromise.

The Cavalier stud dog should be kept in the peak of condition and fed a premium, well-balanced diet that is high in protein to maximize his reproductive abilities. Those who send their bitches for mating have every right to expect that the male is fertile and healthy; therefore a semen analysis should be done on a regular basis to ensure that abundant, healthy, active sperm are present.

Canine brucellosis is a venereal disease that can have catastrophic consequences, such as sterility and fatal deaths. Periodically, the stud dog should have his penis examined for infections and a test run for brucellosis. No stud dog should be bred to a bitch without a current negative brucella test, and active stud dogs should be tested at least twice a year. The bitch should be tested every time before being sent to a stud dog. This disease can be transmitted by other means than breeding, so even virgin animals may carry it. Brucella tests most commonly used today do not have false negatives, but do have false positives from time to time, and if this is the case, a titer must be done. Bitches who are tested in season have a higher incidence of false positives, so having the bitch tested just before she

is expected to be in season is advisable. Having to do a titer may take long enough that the proper time for breeding has gone by before the test result is back. In such cases, if all involved feel fairly sure the positive result is false, breeding by artificial insemination protects the male while avoiding missing the cycle of the bitch. No brucellosis-infected dogs or bitches can be used for breeding, and, at best, those infected must be isolated from

CKCSC, USA and Dutch Champion Jason V.T. Burgstse Hof.
Owned by Daniel and Vanessa Rydholdm.
Photo by Chris Sartre.

A stud dog must be sound physically, mentally and of excellent breed type, without compromise.
CKCSC, USA Champion Dalvreck Dorocha For Flying Colors, 1996 CKCSC, USA National Specialty Winner.
Owned by Cathy Gish. Photo by Michael Allen.

The Cavalier Brood Bitch

Before planning a breeding, the determination must be made that the bitch is worthy of rearing a litter, that is to say, she is healthy in mind, body and of good breed type. She should be from a line of bitches that have no difficulty whelping, and that produce quality, thriving puppies. A bitch should be at least in her second season and older than one year before she is bred, and then only if she is sufficiently mature. It is of paramount importance that a bitch be of the most stable disposition. A nervous, high-strung bitch is not a good candidate for motherhood, because she will transmit this insecurity to her young. A bitch should never be bred on more than two consecutive seasons, as she needs time to recuperate from the physical strain of bearing and rearing her pups. The average Cavalier bitch will take eight months to a year to come back in to full coat and be ready again for the show ring.

When you are planning to breed a bitch on her next season, check her stool sample and treat her for worms if necessary. Vaccinations should be updated three months before a planned breeding. The bitch should have a complete physical examination before being sent to the stud dog, including having a cervical culture run to check for bacterial infections and to check for vaginal abnormalities. We have had several bitches presented to us for breeding over the years that have either had intact hymens or vaginal strictures. Either of these can make a successful breeding difficult or impossible. The bitch should be in excellent physical condition before being bred, and this includes not being overweight!

The Season

The first season of a Cavalier bitch is usually between six and eight months. This season seems to have the heaviest flow and to last the longest. Seasons of Cavalier bitches usually last a full three weeks. First the vulva becomes swollen, followed by a dark, bloody discharge that gradually lightens to a straw color as the bitch enters her

all other dogs. There is no known cure. A negative brucellosis test is never wrong.

It is the obligation of the stud-dog owner to provide a high level of care for the bitch while she is in residence at the stud dog owner's kennel. The stud fee is generally payable at the time of mating unless prior arrangements have been made. Upon payment, the owner of the stud dog should give the bitch owner a stud service certificate, signed and dated.

Male Cavalier puppies may start "practicing" as young as five weeks of age, and it is important they not be scolded for this behavior, as scolding may make them reluctant to breed at maturity. A young male should be trained from the beginning to be handled during mating. It may be necessary to aid with a mating from time to time, and if the male is used to being handled, it will not put him off his stride when intervention is required.

fertile period—usually day eight or nine. The vulva will become very soft and spongy to the touch, and the bitch will become flirtatious. All coy behavior goes out of the window, because the Cavalier bitch is usually an enthusiastic participant in the mating game. She will prance and dance, literally inviting the object of her affections to join in the fun, flirting with other females before she is ready to be actually mated.

Much as you may like to think that your Cavalier darlings are not really dogs, this is the time when you realize, perhaps reluctantly, that they are!

When the bitch is ready to receive the male, she will stand with her back legs planted firmly, tail thrown to one side. Sometimes she will leap away and spin around when mounted, then the game starts over again until she gives in. The exception to this is when a bitch is frightened and is therefore unreceptive. Unless a progesterone test or a vaginal cytology is done, it is easy to miss the right time to breed a bitch with this behavior. Some bitches indicate that they will be receptive, but when the male mounts them, they clamp their vaginal muscles so tightly that the male cannot possibly penetrate. Artificial insemination is the only option.

After the fertile period is over, the vulva will gradually lose its swelling, but the scent of the bitch will continue to attract males for at least another week. It is therefore important that you continue to keep the bitch away from males during this time, to prevent the possibilty of an accidental breeding.

Because of the distance that most Cavalier bitches have to travel for stud service and the expense involved, it is desirable to know the ideal day to breed for the best conception rate and litter size. This is accomplished by having a veterinarian who is familiar with the procedure and interpretation of the results, do a progesterone test on the bitch. This test should be run at least twice. It involves drawing and testing blood while the bitch is in the first week of her season, starting at approximately day four. The cells of the vagina look quite different when a bitch is in her fertile period, which is why a vaginal cytology (smear) is

It is paramount importance that a bitch be of the most stable disposition. CKCSC, USA Champion Mavourneen Hop Skip and A Jump. Bred and owned by Betsey Lynch. Photo by Jan Wendell.

useful although not nearly as accurate as a progesterone test. Bitches can conceive if bred a few days before their fertile period, although a breeding that occurs too early may result in a lack of conception or reduced litter size, as few of the sperm are still alive when the eggs are ready to be fertilized.

When a progesterone test is run and hormone levels indicate that the bitch is entering her fertile period, receptive or not, she must be bred! In the case of a bitch that is reluctant during her fertile period, artificial insemination may be necessary for conception to be achieved

If there is concern about transporting the bitch to the stud dog, fresh chilled or frozen semen is an option. The semen of the male can be collected when the veterinarian determines that a bitch is ready to breed. It is then suspended in a shipping medium, chilled, and shipped overnight to the inseminating veterinarian who will almost immediately artificially inseminate the bitch. Frozen semen is collected earlier and suspended in a medium before being frozen. These specimens

CKCSC, USA Champion Fair Oaks Fairfield Poseidon, owned by Chuck Minter. Shown winning the 1994 CKCSC, USA National Specialty with Judge George Donaldson of Scotland. Photo by Meager.

are frequently from valuable stud dogs that have since deceased. Again, the bitch is artificially inseminated.

Mating

For conventional breeding, the bitch should be sent to the stud dog a few days before she is due to be bred so that she can settle down and become used to her new surroundings. We always use the same room for breeding our Cavaliers so that the males know that he is there for business. The floor should be washable and non-slippery, and the room should be free from disturbance. Neither dog nor bitch should be fed within an hour or so of mating. The dog and bitch should not be left to breed unsupervised, because the bitch could become frightened and hurt the male. They should be allowed to become acquainted before the mating takes place, during which time they will jump and play, ears high on their heads, with a silly expression on their faces.

After allowing a little time for courting, apply a small amount of (non-spermicidal—read the fine print!) lubricating gel to the vulva of the bitch. If there is a height disparity, it is helpful to put something under the back legs of the bitch or dog to make the bitches vulva a height easily

accessible to the male. After the male penetrates and his initial thrusting is over, the gland (bulbus glandis) at the base of the penis will begin to swell inside the bitch. At this point, the male and the bitch will be unable to separate. This is called a tie, which can last anywhere from a few minutes to an hour. Some bitches yelp loudly, and others are quite nonchalant, but after the first few minutes, most accept the inevitable and stand quietly. A tie is not necessary for conception. We once had friends bring a bitch to us for breeding and we could only get an "outside" tie, from which she had five puppies. An outside tie is when the male penetrates, but the bulbus glandis is on the outside of the vagina. This requires the mating pair to be held together while the male ejaculates.

Pregnancy

A pregnant bitch should be fed a natural diet that is a 25 to 30 percent protein diet, increasing the amount of food offered by 1.1 to 1.5 times during the last trimester. Bitches that become picky eaters during the last part of pregnancy should be offered small amounts of food at frequent intervals. Do not supplement a bitch with extra calcium during pregnancy. This can cause the parathyroid glands to become largely inactive, so that when body calcium is needed during whelping and lactation, the parathyroid glands are unable to respond suitably. As a result, the blood calcium will drop to a dangerously low level, leading to uterine inertia and/or eclampsia. Save the high-calcium diet for after whelping when the bitch is nursing her puppies! A daily vitamin tablet may be given.

Is She or Isn't She?

Cavaliers usually have easy pregnancies. For the first five weeks it may be hard to tell if a bitch is in whelp, which can be a time of suspense for the anxious owner. Some of the changes that can occur in early pregnancy are sleepiness, going off of food, and even moodiness. For those who can't wait to find out, a sonogram can be done to tell if the bitch has conceived at twenty-one days after breeding, or a veterinarian can palpate for puppies between twenty-five and twenty-eight days after breeding. There are also canine home pregnancy tests coming on the market.

The average litter size is four puppies. The most vulnerable period for the puppies in utero is fifteen to forty days after breeding, which is when the various organ systems differentiate (males, females, etc.). Be extremely cautious about giving any medications at any time when a bitch is in whelp, but even more so during this period. About five weeks post breeding, a clear sticky discharge from the vagina may be noticed, and mammary glands begin to develop. By five to five and a half weeks, the waistline will thicken and the tummy will get a definite bulge. She may be wormed at this time with a wormer that is safe for pregnant animals, such as Panacur. Never vaccinate a pregnant bitch. The bitch should be kept in good physical condition but not be allowed to over-exert.

Puppies are viable fifty-six days after ovulation, with most Cavalier bitches whelping between fifty-nine and sixty-three days after they were bred. An X-ray can be taken during the last week of pregnancy to determine the number of puppies, but waiting until the fifty-eighth or fifty-ninth day is recommended, because the bones of the puppies will be calcified by then so are more easily seen on film. The normal temperature of a dog is 101.5 to 102.5, but this can drop as low as 98 degrees twelve to twenty-four hours before whelping—the first sign that whelping is imminent. Take the bitch's temperature rectally morning and evening beginning on day fifty-six. Encourage her to sleep in the whelping box a week or so before she is due, or the puppies may be born on your bed!

A litter of three is slightly less than average—pictured at 5 weeks. Photo by Vicki Roach.

Be Prepared

Be prepared for the whelping ahead of time. Post the veterinarian's number by the telephone, and have an easily understandable book about canine reproduction conveniently located for quick reference. I recommend Canine Reproduction. A Breeder's Guide by Phyllis Holst, DVM. Set up a warm, draft-free room with everything that you will need within reach.

- Build or purchase a whelping box and have it clean and ready. There are excellent plastic whelping boxes on the market that are warm, sanitary, and easy to clean. The whelping box should have a "pig rail" so that the bitch cannot squash the newborns against the side of the box.

- A shallow cardboard box with a heating pad (turned on low) or a hot-water bottle should be ready to keep newborns warm until the last puppy is born.

- A stack of clean newspapers, which makes practical bedding before, during, and after whelping, should be placed near the whelping box.

- A plastic garbage bag for the disposal of the soiled newspapers.

- An antiseptic hand wash.

- A stack of clean towels for drying puppies.

- A scale and a notepad to weigh and record puppy birth weights.

- A clock for timing births.

- A sterilized surgical clamp (hemostat), iodine, sharp scissors, and dental floss for tying umbilical cords.

- A suction bulb for the removal of mucus from the mouth or throat of a puppy.

- Oxytocin (which promotes uterine contractions) and doxapram hydrochloride (which stimulates respiration) should be available, if your vet will allow, as well as needles and syringes for their administration. *Note: Oxytocin is a powerful drug and should only be used with the direction of a veterinarian.*

- High calorie paste, such as Nutri-cal.

- A flashlight.

- A leash.

Stage One

Just before the due date, the bitch may be given a bath and have the feathers trimmed around her vulva and down her back legs. A bitch that has previously whelped often has a waxy black buildup on her nipples that is difficult to remove with shampoo. Rub the nipples with a little baby oil, then gently scrub with a soft brush and an antibacterial soap. Rinse thoroughly. *Never* leave a Cavalier bitch alone when she is showing signs of labor, because she may need assistance, and at the very least will simply want to know that you are there. After her temperature drops, she will display the first signs of labor, which are restlessness, panting, and nesting. Occasionally these signs are exhibited before the temperature drop, but this is uncommon. The first stage labor signs can continue for up to twenty-four hours before stage two begins. The bitch should be examined by a veterinarian if labor has not started after that time. Sometimes the bitch will vomit, and she will certainly want to eliminate frequently. This is when she may try to find a hiding place under the house, so take her outside only on a leash and with a flashlight in hand if it is dark. Cavalier bitches most often go into labor at night, so be prepared for an all-night vigil.

. . . .

Active Labor

The second stage of labor is active labor itself, which is when the uterus contracts, expelling the puppy through the cervix into the vagina. A puppy should arrive within one to two hours after the onset of strong contractions. The bitch should break the sac in which the puppy is born, but if she does not, you must do it for her immediately so that the puppy can breathe. Sometimes it is necessary to tear the umbilical cord, and do tear it, rather than cutting it with scissors, as bleeding will be reduced. After the puppy is separated from the bitch, momentarily apply a surgical clamp to the stump of the cord, a small distance from the abdomen of the puppy. Tie the umbilicus off with dental floss to prevent bleeding, and douse it with an iodine solution to prevent infection. If the bitch worries the umbilical stump and makes it bleed, put a bandaid over it, but be sure to remove the bandaid within twenty-four hours. If you wish, dewclaws can be removed at this time.

One day old puppies.
Photo by Diane Gee.

Breech Presentation

Cavalier puppies are often born hind feet first and occasionally get stuck. If this happens, it will be necessary to assist in the delivery. In assisted deliveries, cleanliness is essential, because you don't want to introduce infection into the bitch. Make the bitch stand up, and, if possible, have a second person hold her head. Grasp as much of the puppy as you can with a paper towel, a dry terry washcloth, or anything else that will give you a grip, and pull the puppy downward toward the back feet of the bitch, at the same time working the puppy from side to side. When the puppy is born, if he is not breathing, grasp him firmly and, holding the puppy head first, swing him in an arc toward your feet several times to help clear mucus from the throat or lungs. Rub him vigorously, and be prepared to give mouth-to-nose resuscitation if necessary. If the puppy is breathing in gasps after all passages have been cleared and if the veterinarian has supplied doxapram hydrochloride, give one or two drops on the tongue, which will stimulate respiration.

. . . .

Keep the Puppies Warm

Bitches often don't pay a lot of attention to their newborns when more are on the way. If the bitch will allow, encourage newborns to nurse, which causes natural oxytocin to be released, and in turn, stimulates contractions. After the puppy has nursed, is dry and has his umbilical cord tied off, place him in the box with the heating pad and cover him lightly to keep him warm. If the bitch will not allow the puppy to nurse, or is too restless for safety, put the puppy in the box with the heating pad anyway. It will not hurt the puppy not to nurse for even a few hours if necessary. Warmth is of critical importance to the newborn, as chilling is a major cause of infant mortality in puppies. After the last puppy is born, the bitch will usually have a marked change in behavior, and will look anxiously for her new family.

English, CKCSC, USA and Canadian Champion
Sukev Dolly Daydream of Laughing.
Owned by the author. Photo by Fall.

Care of the Bitch While Whelping

When a delivery is long, the bitch will become tired. An inch of a high calorie paste such as Nutri-Cal will give her a good boost between puppies and after whelping. Fresh water must also be offered from time to time (we offer our bitches a cup of warm tea with sugar!) When the whelping is protracted, the bitch must be put on a leash and taken outside to relieve herself. Carry a flashlight with you as well as a towel so that you are prepared in case of an unexpected arrival.

Each puppy born will have a placenta. Accounting for these can be tricky, because the bitch may eat one while you are not looking. You need to be sure that none have been retained by the bitch, because this can cause infection which could be life-threatening. A shot of oxytocin given twenty-four hours after whelping will help the bitch expel any retained placentas and leftover debris. We allow our bitches to eat one of the placentas, but eating more than one can cause her to have diarrhea.

DANGER SIGNS AND WHEN TO CALL YOUR VET

Don't hesitate to call the vet for help if you suspect that your bitch may be in trouble. Never was the phrase "better safe than sorry," more appropriate than during whelping.

Call the vet when:

- Second-stage labor has not started twenty-four hours after the temperature drop.

- There is a greenish black discharge before any puppies are born.

- There is a foul-smelling discharge, or the dripping of more than a small amount of pure blood.

- More than two hours have passed since the first contraction was seen and no puppy has arrived.

- Heavy contractions and straining with no puppy after thirty minutes.

- More than six hours between puppies and it is obvious that there are more to be born.

- If a puppy is stuck and cannot be dislodged.

- If you are not comfortable with the way things are progressing.

Complications

Cavaliers are not always problem free when it comes to whelping. The following are the most frequent complications.

Uterine Inertia

Primary uterine inertia occurs when the bitch goes into labor normally and whelping does not progress past stage one. Secondary uterine inertia occurs when the uterine muscles become exhausted and need assistance to continue. Either case will require a veterinarian to administer calcium intravenously, as well as oxytocin. If these remedies do not work, a caesarean section is the only resort.

Caesarean Sections

Occasionally, a bitch will not be able to give birth because a puppy is too large, the bitch's pelvic opening is too small, or some type of blockage or uterine inertia occurs. In these circumstances a Caesarean section or surgical delivery must be performed.

Cavaliers do well with Caesarean sections and are usually nursing their puppies normally within twelve hours. Check daily to see that the stitches of the bitch are clean, dry and uninfected until their removal after ten days.

One of our bitches had a caesarean section a few years ago, and when the puppies were a week old, both her internal and external stitches came undone. Thankfully, I happened to be in the kitchen when she yelped, and I went over to see why. I stood frozen in horror as I saw a large mass begin to protrude from her abdomen. I had no idea what to do, but I knew that I had to do something fast. I gathered the bitch and her insides into the loose shirt that I was wearing and started shrieking for Bob. Bob wrapped plastic wrap around her abdomen to keep her wound clean and moist, after which we got to the vet in record time. She was surgically repaired and suffered no ill effects.

Postwhelping Complications

Acute Metritis

Sometimes if a bitch has had a long, hard labor or has a retained placenta, she can get an infected uterus, or metritis. Trust your instincts— you know your bitch and can tell better than anyone when something is wrong! A raging infection can result in spaying or possibly death if metritis is not treated aggressively. If the bitch seems unusually dull, has trouble walking, has a fever, or does not want to stay with her puppies. Contact your veterinarian immediately.

Eclampsia

Eclampsia, or milk fever, is caused by low blood calcium levels, and can occur during the first three to four weeks after whelping. It often occurs when small dogs have large litters. Symptoms include restlessness, anxiety, rapid breathing, whining, and eventually, uncoordinated movement and convulsions. The bitch must be treated immediately with intravenous calcium, and nursing of the puppies must be restricted.

We had a bitch who had always been the most trouble-free of mothers. One frigid January morning she woke me up fussing to go outside. When she came back in, I knew that something was wrong, because she was restless, kept rubbing her head on the carpet, and did not want to go back in the nest with her puppies. We bundled her up and drove down the mountain to the vet, who gave her some calcium, and started home an hour later.

By this time, the weather had turned into a full blizzard, complete with slippery roads and poor visibility. When we finally got home, I put the bitch back with her puppies, but in no time she was out of the nest again, trembling, eyes glazing. Her temperature had soared and she was beginning to convulse. I rushed to the phone to call our neighbor for help and thought that I was explaining the situation clearly enough, asking him if he would drive us down the mountain in his four-wheel-drive truck. Within minutes, there was a blare of sirens and flashing lights as an ambulance came tearing down the driveway. Our neighbor, unable to imagine that I could get so excited about a dog, thought that I was talking about my husband. The ambulance drivers were most understanding and, thanks to them, we got to the vet just in time!

. . . .

Mastitis

If the puppies do not consume all of the milk produced, the bitches teats will often become hard, tender and compacted—this necessitates gently massaging her teats and milking her by hand. Hot compresses will often loosen the milk and make expressing it easier. Be aware that this milk could make the puppies ill, The affected teats should be drained completely.

. . . .

Pyometra (not necessarily associated with breeding)

Pyometra is a life-threatening disease of the uterus that requires urgent veterinary attention. The uterus becomes filled with pus, and if the cervix is closed, spaying is the only solution. With an open cervix, treating the bitch with prostaglandins and the drug Batryl can be successful. Signs can include a swollen abdomen, excessive thirst and urination, and, in the case of an open cervix, a pinkish green discharge. This is most common in the older bitches and usually occurs thirty to sixty days after the last heat season or after whelping. In the case of a "closed" pyometra, when the cervix is not open and cannot discharge, toxic shock syndrome can result—which can quickly be fatl. It is best to spay bitches when they are no longer going to be used for breeding.

The least known attribute of the Cavalier is its hunting instinct.
Lily, Julie and Tootsie, owned and photographed by Chris Mankofsky.

chapter twelve

RAISING A LITTER

$\mathcal{A}$ Cavalier bitch makes a wonderful mother. A secluded corner of the family room or kitchen is an ideal spot for a bitch and her babies, as although she will be very protective of her puppies, she won't like to be shut away from her family while she raises them. At first a bitch may be reluctant to leave her puppies long enough to eat, drink, or go outside. She may need more tempting meals and sometimes may even need to be hand fed and hand watered; in fact, she needs and deserves to be pampered. If a bitch will not voluntarily go outside to eliminate, she must be made to do so. Don't be surprised if she has a little diarrhea for the first few days, this is not unusual after whelping, especially if several placentas have been eaten. Kaopectate will usually settle things down. If the hair around the vulva was clipped prior to whelping, keeping the bitch clean will be easy, but any feces or discharge that remains on her feathers should be rinsed off with warm water before the bitch returns to her nest. The bitch will have a discharge after the puppies are born, sometimes containing a small amount of blood, but this should clear up in a few days. A smelly

The average sized litter is four puppies. Eight week old Chadwick puppies. Photo by Anne Robins

discharge or copious bleeding are signs of danger, and immediate veterinary attention should be sought.

While a bitch is nursing her puppies, she may need three to four times her normal amount of food, which should be high in both fat and protein. She will need it divided into several meals a day.

Care of the Puppies

The first seventy-two hours are the most critical time for newborns. Puppies have no ability to control their temperature when they are very young, so it is important that they are in a warm, draft-free place. Temperature-controlled heating pads are made especially for whelping boxes, which are recommended over the use of heat lamps, which can cause the bitch to get too hot. Overheating puppies can also be dangerous, so if you use a conventional heating pad, be certain that the setting is on low.

The whelping box must be kept clean and dry. Newspapers make good bedding, although the puppies will take on a gray tinge from the newsprint. It is not safe to use blankets with newborn puppies, because the mother may roll them into the blanket and asphyxiate the puppies accidentally.

Puppies need to be stimulated in order to eliminate for the first few days, but new mothers do not always know that they should do this. Check to see if there is fecal matter under the tails of the puppies, and if there is, remove it gently with cotton wool that has been dampened with warm water, dabbing gently in the appropriate place to make the puppies urinate and defecate. The bitch will usually take over eventually.

Puppies should look plump and round. The best sound of a healthy litter is no sound other than the gurgles and slurps that accompany vigorous nursing. A puppy crying continuously indicates trouble, so never disregard it. One that is doing poorly and that has milk bubbling from the nose may have a cleft palate and if so, should be euthanized. In the case of a large litter, make sure that the small puppies get a turn at the milk bar. If the smaller puppies look thin, remove the bigger

ones to a warm box several times a day in order to let the little ones have a good nurse on their own. Weak puppies are helped by 1cc of glucose mixed with an electrolyte solution (such as Pediolyte) two or three times daily until they get stronger.

Occasionally a puppy will be born that just does not thrive. I don't know of any Cavalier breeder who does not go to heroic efforts to keep a puppy alive, but hard as you might try, puppies that do not thrive from birth almost always die. In a situation such as this, do everything possible, give it your best try, but do it with the knowledge that the battle will most likely be lost.

Sexing Puppies

Ridiculous as it may sound, I have had people call and ask how they can tell. So here's how!

It's a BOY!

It's a GIRL!

Bottle Feeding

Small puppies may need to have supplemental feedings, and there are tiny nursing bottles and excellent formulas that are made especially for this purpose. Goat's milk diluted in half with bottled water is suitable if a formula is not obtainable. Care must be taken when feeding a

puppy, because if milk gets into the lungs, pneumonia can result. The head of a puppy should never be tilted back when bottle feeding, but rather held slightly above level.

Tube Feeding

Tube feeding is an option when a puppy needs supplemental feeding, but must be done with caution because it entails slipping a tube down the puppy's throat into his stomach. A veterinarian should explain the procedure, and it is important to work with someone who knows how to tube feed before you try to do it on your own. Tube feeding can be fatal if it is not done properly.

Do not overfeed puppies when supple-menting, too much food can cause diarrhea. Read the directions on the can or box. Warning: some commercially prepared supplements may cause cataracts, so read labels and follow directions exactly.

Optional Tail Docking and Dewclaw Removal

Cavalier puppies should have their dewclaws removed in their first week, which may

be done by a veterinarian. If tails are to be docked, they are usually docked at three days of age, not removing more than one-third. Nothing looks worse than a tail that has been docked too short. Where applicable, be sure to leave a white tip.

Physical and mental capacities develop so quickly that puppies are stimulated by human handling and the sound of a radio, squeaky toys, and games. After the first few days, puppies should be handled gently on a daily basis, tickling tummies, rubbing paws, and speaking to them quietly. This time spent socializing them is of enormous importance, as their temperaments develop quickly. Eyes open at ten to fifteen days and they begin to hear at about the same time. They soon begin to follow things with their eyes and recognize littermates. They will explore their environment and begin to play with littermates at about four weeks. Start trimming their nails at this age, and continue to trim them every two weeks thereafter, to prevent the mother's teats from becoming sore. Puppies are instinctively clean and will leave their bed to do their business as far away as possible. Early on start to designate part of the nest as bed, with bedding that is preferably something the mother cannot rumple-up—and part as bathroom with newspaper.

Once puppies get the idea, they will get right in the dish and eat enthusiastically. Photo by Chris Mankofsky.

It is important not to separate a puppy from his littermates too early, because it is here that he learns life in society, where he will discover his strengths and weaknesses. Puppies learn much by play fighting and quickly realize that their sharp teeth cause pain. They know that one must not annoy another one without good reason. The dam, who can be quite stern, doesn't hesitate to instill in her puppies the respect that she considers her due. Deprived of an important part of early education, the puppy will never be at ease in canine or human society.

Worms

Puppies are often born with round-worms. Even though a bitch is de-wormed before she is bred, de-worming medication is not effective against dormant larvae that has become encysted in the tissue and have become active due to the stress of whelping. Puppies should be wormed for the first time at three weeks of age, and again at six and nine weeks. Alternatively, have the veterinarian run a stool sample on the puppies. Another stool sample should be run again when the puppy is four to six months of age.

Weaning

Puppies can be introduced to food between three and a half and five weeks of age. Finely grind the puppy food in a blender, then mix it with warm goat's milk or warm water to make a gruel. Goat's milk, which can be purchased in cans, frozen, or fresh, is an excellent food source for the puppies. It is high in calcium and phosphorus and is easily digested. The ground-up food will take a surprising amount of fluid to make it into a lapping consistency, and when it has sat for a few minutes, it will probably need even more fluid added. Pour the gruel into a shallow dish—a pie plate, for instance. Before giving the food to the puppies, remove the mother from the nest or she will be into it before they have a chance! Sometimes it is necessary to dip a puppy's nose into the food or put a little on a fingertip to start a puppy eating. Once given the idea, the puppies will more than likely get right into the dish and eat enthusiastically. You will discover that Cavalier mothers make excellent walking napkins when the meal is over!

Weaning should be completed by six-and-a-half weeks. Start by removing the bitch from the nest for a few hours at four and a half weeks, then for the day, then completely. It is not good for a bitch to become run down by letting her puppies nurse for longer than necessary. Once her milk is dried up, which usually takes about a week, the bitch may have her puppies back. A bitch should not be deprived of this time with her puppies, because it is important for her to play with them, and teach them social behavior. The puppies may still nurse, but it is for security only. The natural method of weaning, that is where the bitch has full access to her puppies at all times and weans them voluntarily, is perhaps easier for the owner, but is undoubtedly harder physically on the bitch, regardless of the amount of food she is given.

One-Puppy Litters

One-puppy litters are not uncommon for Cavalier bitches and can be a task for the owner. A single puppy has all of the milk that he wants without challenge, so he may become overweight and turn into a swimmer puppy. Weaning is problematical, because the puppy has no siblings for company and warmth and therefore requires even more attention than puppies from normal-sized litters. Lots of plushy toys, lots of attention, and lots of one-on-one socializing equals a spoiled, adored puppy, and probably one that will be a part of your family forever!

Problems

Constipation

If the puppy is not nursing, but has a rounded, full stomach, constipation may be the culprit. An enema of 1cc of warm water, injected slowly into the rectum will usually bring relief. If the condition persists, contact a veterinarian.

Cryptorchids

By the time a male puppy is six months old, if both of his testicles have not descended into his scrotum, he is cryptorchid (from the Greek word "kryptos," meaning "hidden"). A dog with no descended testicles is referred to as a bilateral cryptorchid, and although infertile, he will have a normal sex drive. A dog with one normal testicle is referred to as a unilateral cryptorchid. This dog will be fertile. Undescended testicles are more prone to cancer and can lead to serious complications should they become twisted internally. Affected males should be neutered, because undescended testicles are a genetic condition.

Diarrhea

A veterinarian should be consulted immediately if diarrhea develops. Causes may include: viruses, bacteria or protozoan infections, acidic milk from the bitch, and overfeeding. Diarrhea in puppies is always of concern, particularly in the case of newborns, because they can dehydrate and die very quickly. Once a puppy gets run down, it can be difficult, if not impossible, to bring him back to good health, so be vigilant. Dehydration can be recognized by pinching the skin at the base of the tail or neck. If the skin does not immediately fall back into place but remains standing in the pinched position, the puppy is dehydrated. Immediate action must be taken, because the puppy will die if the condition is not treated aggressively. A small amount of Kaopectate will usually help slow down diarrhea, and in an emergency, one drop of Immodium is worth a try. An electrolyte solution, which contains essential minerals present in body fluids, can be purchased from the baby section of a drugstore or supermarket. Very slowly drip one or two drops of the electrolyte solution into the puppy's mouth, taking care not to hold the head much past a horizontal position. A badly dehydrated puppy may need to have fluids injected under his skin every few hours, but this should be done under the direction of a veterinarian. If a puppy is dirty, bathe him in warm water and thoroughly dry him before returning him to the nest.

Fading Puppy Syndrome

A fading puppy is one that does not thrive for a number of reasons. Some of the causes of fading puppies are: low birth weight, birth defects, dam's nipples being too large for the puppy to nurse, insufficient milk, viral or bacterial infections. Good sanitation, which includes sterilizing whelping tools used between litters and keeping the whelping box clean will lessen the chance of septicemia and peritonitis. Herpes virus and Canine Brucellosis, as well as the protozoan Toxoplasmosis may also cause fading puppies.

Hernias

Inguinal Hernias

Inguinal hernias, which are located in the groin, can be dangerous, and it is generally agreed by the veterinary community that if they do not spontaneously close at an early age, they should be surgically repaired. Once repaired, there is nothing to worry about. Affected Cavaliers should not be put into a breeding program, because inguinal hernias can be life-threatening and are considered to be genetic in origin.

Scrotal Hernias

Scrotal hernias, obviously affecting only males, occur when the tube in which the testes descend into the scrotum is too large, allowing intestines to descend into the scrotal canal. This is another situation that can be dangerous, and an affected puppy should be repaired as early as possible. Frequently, the puppy will be neutered at the

same time as the hernia repair, because surgery time is shortened—a particularly important consideration in a young puppy. Again, once the scrotal hernia is repaired, there is no cause for concern.

Umbilical Hernias

Umbilical hernias are quite common in the breed and seldom need repair. Though many breeders persist in believing that they are caused by the bitch pulling too hard to bred the cord at birth, evidence supports the idea that umbilical hernias are also genetic. Cavaliers with umbilical hernias are used for breeding since the problem is not a major health concern, and there are many other more serious genetic health issues to deal with, before these normally harmless hernias become an issue. This type of hernia is most frequently due to the umbilical ring not closing immediately after birth. Sometimes a little fatty tissue is trapped on the outside of the abdomen after the ring closes, leaving a small, hard protrusion. If the protrusion cannot be pushed back up into the abdomen, the hernia is referred to as non-reducible, and it is of no concern, either for health, show, or breeding purposes. If the fatty protrusion continues to be soft and is able to be pushed back up into the abdomen, it is called a reducible hernia. Surgery may be advisable if the abdominal ring has not closed by adulthood, particularly in the case of a bitch that is going to be used for breeding, but again, this is infrequent. In all of the years we have been breeding Cavaliers, we have only had one umbilical hernia repaired.

Herpes

May cause abortion, still born, runted and fading puppies. Symptoms are refusal to eat and continuous crying, along with soft, yellow-green stool. Almost always fatal to puppies under three weeks, there is no known treatment or prevention.

Hypoglycemia

Hypoglycemia (low blood sugar) is not uncommon in Cavalier puppies, but they will usually outgrow this condition by six months unless there is a deeper underlying problem. Caloric intake must be supplemented until normal pathways are working, which is why puppies should be fed three to four times daily through at least four months of age. Hypoglycemia is one of the primary causes of death in newborns.

Open Fontanel

When puppies are young, all of their bones have room for growth, called growth plates. An open fontanel is located in the center of the top of the head and is an open area where the bones have not yet grown together. The fontanel of some Cavalier puppies may be slower to close than others, but it is very unusual for closure not to be completed by a year of age. An open fontanel in a Cavalier puppy rarely means that he is hydrocephalic (water on the brain).

Peritonitis

If the groin area of the puppy is dark and discolored, the puppy will not eat and cries constantly, peritonitis should be suspected. Immediate veterinary attention is required, as the puppy will need antibiotics, both orally and in the abdomen. Often caused by contamination of the umbilical cord.

Pneumonia

Pneumonia can be due to a puppy becoming chilled, from getting fluid in the lungs, or from a viral infection. Labored breathing and a rattling in the chest are sure signs. Antibiotic therapy is required, so get immediate veterinary attention. The puppy must be kept warm and tube fed if he will not nurse.

Puppy Murmurs

It is not uncommon for Cavalier puppies to have a heart murmur for the first few weeks, which

Grantilley That's The Ticket of Bramble at 8 weeks. Owned by Joy Sims, photo by Barbara Augello.

will usually disappear by twelve to fourteen weeks of age. A veterinarian should be able to tell the difference between a puppy murmur and a murmur caused from a faulty heart.

Septicemia

The first indication of septicemia is if the puppy's lips, feet, nose and stomach have turned a bright purplish-red. Septicemia in puppies will be fatal unless the puppies are treated with an antibiotic at the early stage of infection, so immediately seek veterinary help. Usually caused by viruses transmitted to the puppy at birth from a vaginal infection, contamination of the umbilical cord or unclean conditions during and after whelping.

Swimmer Puppies

Also known as flat-puppy syndrome, swimmer puppies resemble turtles, with their legs sticking out to the sides rather than being underneath their bodies. They become quite flat chested from lying on their stomachs. Overweight puppies are much more likely to be swimmers and are frequently found in litters of only one or two. We have had only one swimmer, and other than keeping him on a non-slippery surface (indoor-outdoor carpeting), he grew out of it on his own by eight weeks with no lasting effects. Foam-rubber egg-crate–style mattress pads take the pressure off of the chest and encourage the legs to drop, but this must be discarded at the first signs of the puppy, or mother, chewing the foam rubber. Some breeders place hobbles on swimmer puppies, but because they seem to outgrow it on their own, this is probably unnecessary.

Toxic Milk Syndrome

Occasionally the milk of the bitch will contain bacterial toxins, which can cause her puppies to have severe diarrhea and bloating, which if left untreated, will lead to death. The puppies must be immediately removed from the bitch for twelve to twenty-four hours, and the bitch must receive antibiotic therapy.

THE HEALTHY PUPPY vs. THE SICK PUPPY

A Healthy Puppy	A Sick Puppy
gains weight	doesn't gain weight
looks plump	is flat and limp
has a shiny coat	has diarrhea
seldom cries	cries constantly
nurses vigorously	doesn't nurse
warm to the touch	feels cool to the touch
"active" sleep	lies quietly asleep

Interaction as a young puppy with humans and littermates teaches a puppy about life in society, here he will discover his strengths and weaknesses. Ted Eubank with the Pinecrest Cavaliers. Photo by Shooters.

First two weeks:

- Keep the puppies warm, make sure they are nursing and that the dam is keeping them clean.
- Weigh daily to monitor weight gain, until birth weight is doubled, usually at one week.
- (optional) Remove dew claws and dock tails on day three.
- Eyes open at ten - 12 days.
- Puppy begins to hear at approximately two weeks.

Third and fourth weeks:

- Trim nails.
- Puppies begin to toddle and play.
- Handle puppies gently, rubbing tummies and feet.
- Introduce water and food of a lappable consistency.
- Worm if necessary.
- Remove dam from puppies for a short period.

Fifth and sixth weeks:

- Trim nails.
- Socialization with humans very important from this time on.
- Introduce moistened puppy food.
- At five and one-half weeks, remove dam from puppies during the day, but allow her to be with her puppies at night.
- First vaccinations given at six weeks, and every three weeks through four months.
- *Six to six and one- half weeks, wean puppies completely. Feed 3-4 times daily, and have clean water available at all times.*

Seventh and eighth weeks:

- Trim nails.
- Allow mother back with her puppies to play.
- Worm if necessary.
- Early training and housebreaking begins.
- Thorough check up by veterinarian before leaving for new home after eighth week birthday.

Stages of Development

Cavaliers go through several stages of development. By three months of age, they often enter into what is a gawky adolescent stage, when they are leggy, lanky, and awkward. Some never go through this period, while others make their owners despair. Sometimes the only hope is that basic bone structure doesn't change—a puppy that is well-constructed at eight weeks will grow into a well-constructed adult.

As young puppies, Cavaliers use their tails for balance, so their tail carriage may be questionable. Toplines change with alarming regularity. Heads, which were so pretty as babies, may seem domed and unfilled in the muzzle. Bites may go off, and it seems to take forever for the full coat to come in. Some youngsters attain their full height as early as six months, or the reverse may happen and they look light in bone.

Canadian Champion Salador Coogan as a graduate puppy. Owned by Shelia Smith, England. Photo by Smith.

Coogan as an adult, before being imported to Canada by Garrett Lambert. Photo by David Bull.

Do not despair! It may take a year and a half to two years for the adolescent Cavalier to fulfill his promise, but it can be well worth the wait.

CKCSC, USA and Canadian Champion Laughing Charisma, owned and bred by the author.
Age six weeks. Photo by the author.

Charisma at one year. Photo by Vavra.

Charisma at four years old after winning the 1993 CKCSC, USA National Specialty. Photo by Vavra.

English Canadian and CKCSC, USA Champion Alansmere Rhett Butler.
Owned and cherished by the author. Photo by Fall.

chapter thirteen

NOTEWORTHY CAVALIERS

CKCSC, USA, Canadian, Mexican, Americas and World Champion Rocky Racoon of Wyndcrest • CKCSC, USA, Canadian and Bermuda Champion Kindrum Byron of Tarryon • CKCSC, USA and Canadian Champion Maxholt Special Secret of Chadwick • CKCSC, USA Champion Ravenrush Tartan • CKCSC, USA Champion B.J. Holy Terror • CKCSC, USA and Canadian Champion Rutherford Elliot of Shagbark • CKCSC, USA, Canadian, Bermuda, SKC and CDA Champion, U-UD Maxholt Special Love Story, UDX, Can/Ber OTCh, SKC UD, CDA CD, TT, CGC • CKCSC, USA and AKC Champion Luxxar Deep Ellum • CKCSC, USA and AKC Champion Partridge Wood Laughing Misdemeanour • CKCSC, USA and AKC Champion Grantilley English Rose at Laughing • Canadian Champion Pixyline Ivory Coast • Canadian Champion Peatland Dasher • CKCSC, USA and Canadian Champion Amantra Naval Salute • Canadian Champion Salador Celtic Dirk • CKCSC, USA and Canadian Champion Roydwood Royal Mail • Canadian and Bermuda Champion Mostyn Spencer For Hire, Can/Ber CDX • Canadian Champion Muffity Fi-Fi • Canadian Champion Kewpy's Bo Diddley • Canadian and AKC Champion Happy Boy of Fairytale Forest • Canadian and AKC Champion Mostyn Celtic Sorin

The Cavaliers named here are not the only noteworthy Cavaliers by any means, they are just a representative few from Canada and the United States. The ten selected for each country were either top winning show dogs, outstanding producers and often times, both.

Rocky

Photo by Letterly

CKCSC, USA , Can., Mex., Am., World Ch. Rocky Raccoon of Wyndcrest.

Blenheim Dog
Bred in Canada by Olivia Darbyshire and D. Hendriks
Owned by Harold and Joan Letterly, Wyndcrest Cavaliers

Rocky won BIS at three Rare Breed shows and three BISS, including the CKCSC, USA National Specialty in 1983. He sired 35 champions, some of which are BISS winners in their own right. Rocky's legacy continues in his grand-children and great-grandchildren, one of the best known being the Klingler's CKCSC, USA and Can. Ch. Magnolia's Southern Belle of Wyndcrest.

Xmas Cracker of Amantra

Can. Ch. Amantra Pinball Wizard

Amantra Gypsy Girl

CKCSC, USA, Can., Mex., Am., World Ch. Rocky Raccoon of Wyndcrest

Can. Ch. Kindrum Sparrow

Can. Ch. Kbert Jenny Wren

Can. Ch. Kindrum Louise

Byron

CKCSC, USA, Can., Ber. Ch. Kindrum Byron of Tarryon.

Blenheim Dog
Bred by Mrs. Pam Thornhill, England
Owned by Mr. and Mrs. David Burnham,
Tarryon Cavaliers and Mr. David Rubin

Byron won the CKCSC, USA National Specialty in 1984, 1985, 1986, the only Cavalier to date to accomplish this.

Photo by Rubin

Kindrum Roulette

Kindrum Ludo

Kindrum Candida

CKCSC, USA, Can., Ber. Ch. Kindrum Byron of Tarryon

Kindrum Roulette

Eng. Ch. Kindrum Arabella

Valerius Lotus Blossom

Chelsea

Photo by Robins

CKCSC, USA, Can., Ch. Maxholt Special Secret of Chadwick.

Tricolor Bitch
Bred by Mrs. Peggy Talbot, England
Owned by C. Anne Robins,
Chadwick Cavaliers

An exceptional bitch, "Chelsea" was typical of the best of the Maxholts, and was the top winning Cavalier bitch in the mid-1980s. Her children and grand-children have produced champions, including Denise Quittmeyer's CKCSC, USA Champion Chadwick Great Balls of Fire, who in turn produced CKCSC, USA Champion Chadwick Theatrical Triology and BISS winner, CKCSC, USA Champion Chadwick Tapestry.

Eng. Ch. Maxholt Jack in the Box

Master Dill of Maxholt

Louisa of Shonks

CKCSC, USA, Can. Ch. Maxholt Special Secret of Chadwick

Eng. Ch. Maxholt Christmas Carol

UFO of Maxholt

Lady Candy of Jubilee

CKCSC, USA Ch. B.J. Holy Terror.

Blenheim Dog
Bred and owned by Jo Ann Carvill, B.J. Cavaliers

Record-winning Cavalier in the CKCSC, USA to date, with 20 BISS wins including the CKCSC, USA National Specialty 1991 and 1993. A dog of superb style, type and soundness, Holy Terror is another who has gained international recognition. Some of his get include CKCSC, USA Ch. B.J. Spontaneous Combustion; CKCSC, USA Ch. B.J. Here We Go Again of Roi L; and CKCSC, USA Ch.Flying Colors Kitty Russell.

Photo by Meager

Eng. Ch. Salador Corrigan

CKCSC, USA, Can. Ch. Kindrum Lucifer at Rutherford

Kindrum Flame Lily

CKCSC, USA Ch. B.J. Holy Terror

B.J. Uppity

B.J. Blue Moon

B.J. Quiet Riot

Piccadilly

CKCSC, USA, Can., Ber., SKC, CDA Ch.;U-UD Maxholt Special Love Story, AKC UDX, Can./Ber. OTCh., SKC UD, CDA CD, TT, CGC.

Photo by York

Tricolor Dog
Bred by Mrs. Peggy
Talbot, England
Owned by Janet York,
Piccadil Cavaliers

Holder of five championship titles, five UDs, two OTCh.s, a UDX, and countless HITs. "Piccadilly" was known not only for his breed type, but also for his amazing versatility—he excelled in obedience, hunting, flyball, scent hurdle, agility, canine freestyle ballet, and as a therapy dog.

Eng. Ch. Maxholt Jack in the Box

Master Dill of Maxholt

Louisa of Shonks

CKCSC, USA, Can., Ber., SKC & CDA Ch.; U-UD Maxholt Special Love Story UDX, Can./Ber. OTCh., SKC UD, CDA CD, TT, CGC

Minstrel Boy of Maxholt

Maxholt Love Story

Maxholt Tyreless

Parker

CKCSC, USA, AKC Ch. Luxxar Deep Ellum.

Blenheim Dog
Bred and owned by Paula
Campanozzi, Luxxar Cavaliers

*A dog of ideal type and size,
"Parker" was the youngest
male Cavalier to become a
CKCSC, USA champion. With
many BISS wins, Parker won
BIS the first weekend Cavaliers
went into open competition in
the AKC. He went on to become
the number one Cavalier King
Charles Spaniel in the AKC in
1996, with numerous BOB's and
Toy Group placements.*

Photo by Gay Glazbrook

Can. Ch. Salador Celtic Dirk

CKCSC, USA Ch. Ravenrush Tartan

CKCSC, USA Ch. Montbarle Ceri Mair of Ravenrush

CKCSC, USA, AKC Ch. Luxxar Deep Ellum

CKCSC, USA, AKC Ch. Ravanrush Best Dressed of Luxxar

Ravenrush Haute Couture of Luxxar

CKCSC, USA Ch. Montbarle Ceri Mair of Ravenrush

Photo by Michael Allen

CKCSC, USA, AKC Ch. Partridge Wood Laughing Misdemeanour.

Ruby Bitch
Bred by Deborah King
Owned by Cindy Lazzeroni, Court Cavaliers

Multiple BISS wins as well as numerous BOB's and Toy Group placements. First Cavalier to win Best of Breed at the Westminster Kennel Club show, January 1997. Top Ruby winning Ruby bitch to date in the US, both CKCSC, USA and AKC.

Eng. Ch. Salador Crismark

CKCSC, USA, Can. Ch. Laughing Charisma

Eng., Can., CKCSC, USA Ch.. Sukev Dolly Daydream at Laughing

CKCSC, USA, AKC Ch. Partridge Wood Laughing Misdemeanour

CKCSC, USA Ch. Kindrum Redcoat of Ravenrush

Laughing Must Be Magic

Downsbank Blackberry at Laughing

La Liz

CKCSC, USA, AKC Ch. Grantilley English Rose at Laughing.

Blenheim Bitch
Bred by Rita Bidgood, England
Owned by Barbara Garnett Smith,
Laughing Cavaliers

A bitch of exceptional type and true toy spaniel size, at three years old, "La Liz" is the record-winning CKCSC, USA bitch to date, with 14 BISS wins thus far.

Photo by Digital Artistry

Homerbrent Harry at Stonepit

Robrook Flash Harry

Bleakmoor Emily at Robrook

CKCSC, USA, AKC Ch. Grantilley English Rose at Laughing

Keelham Jamie at Lillico

Rosie Quartz of Grantilley

Grantilley Reflection

Tucker

CKCSC, USA Ch. Ravenrush Tartan.

Blenheim Dog
Bred and owned by Messrs. Gammon and Schroll,
Ravenrush Cavaliers

A multiple Best in Show winner, including the CKCSC, USA National Specialty 1990. One of the most significant sires to come along in recent years, "Tucker" sired numerous champions who themselves have sired champions. Some of offspring include CKCSC, USA and AKC Ch. Luxxar Deep Ellum; CKCSC, USA and AKC Ch. Ravenrush Gillespie and AKC Ch. Ravenrush Impresario. Deep Ellum and Gillespie are both multiple CKCSC, USA BISS winners and all three are AKC BIS winners.

(Photo not provided)

Eng. Ch. Salador Celtic Prince

Can. Ch. Salador Celtic Dirk

Eng. Ch. Salador Colleen

CKCSC, USA Ch. Ravenrush Tartan

Eng. Ch. Salador Corrigan

CKCSC, USA Ch. Montbarle Ceri Mair of Ravenrush

Montbarle Marie Louise

Basil

CKCSC, USA, Can. Ch. Rutherford Elliot of Shagbark.

Tricolor male.
Bred by Roberta Jones
Owned by Martha Guimond, Shagbark Cavaliers.

Another exceptionally good producer, "Basil" sired a number of champion offspring, who have sired champion offspring themselves. Some of his better known get have been the prepotent sire Ch. Ravenrush Best Dressed of Luxxar, the litter sisters CKCSC, USA Ch. Redthea Poppycock of Applegate and CKCSC, USA Ch. Redthea Appleblossom of Applegate and the winner of the 1997 CKCSC, USA National Specialty and Multiple BISS winner CKCSC, USA and AKC Ch. Sheeba Special Edition.

(Photo not provided)

Eng. Ch. Salador Celtic Prince

Can. Ch. Salador Celtic Dirk

Eng. Ch. Salador Colleen

CKCSC, USA, Can. Ch. Rutherford Elliot of Shagbark

Kindrum Cardinal Red

Can. Ch. Kindrum Alice at Rutherford

Kindrum Matilda of Biscay

Photo courtesy Watkins

Can. Ch. Pixyline
Ivory Coast.

Tricolor Dog
Bred by June Huggon,
England
Owned by Dave and Gloria
Watkins, Castlewood
Cavaliers

Top winning Cavalier in Canada and number three Toy in 1980, a record which stood for fifteen years.

Bonnyglen Jasper of Blagreaves

Eng. Ch. Homaranne Andy Capp

Eng. Ch. Homerbrent Captivation

Can. Ch Pixyline Ivory Coast

Homerbrent Henry

Dill of High Head

Homaranne Tammy Lin

Dasher

Can. Ch. Peatland Dasher.

Blenheim Dog. Bred by Mary Millican, England
Owned by Mrs. Angela Thomas,
Charlemere Cavaliers

Winner of both the Canadian and CKCSC, USA National Specialties in 1981 and 1982 respectively. Top Cavalier in Canada, 1981, with many Toy Group wins. Sire and grandsire of many Canadian champions, including the BISS winning siblings by CKCSC, USA and Canadian Ch. Laughing Charisma, and Charisma's son and daughter, Canadian Ch. Charlemere Headliner and Canadian Ch. Charlemere Canadian Colors. Dasher sired his last litter of six puppies at 13 1/2 years and lived to be 15 1/2. It was said of him that "he never missed a bitch and he never missed a meal"!

Photo by Thomas

Eng. Ch. Homaranne Andy Capp

Homerbrent Flash Harry

Eng. Ch. Homerbrent Lindy Lou

Can. Ch. Peatland Dasher

Farne Silver Shadow of McGoogans

Pantisa Saab

Pantisa Merle

Skipper

CKCSC, USA, Can. Ch. Amantra Naval Salute.

Blenheim Dog
Bred by Mrs. D. Fry,
England
Owned by Christine Gingell,
Cuariadd Cavaliers

Many BOB's and Toy Group placements, also a Canadian BIS winner. A CKCSC, USA BISS winner including the CKCSC, USA National Specialty 1987 and the CKCSC, USA Silver Jubilee.

Photo by Callea

Amantra Naval Encounter

Eng. Ch. Naval Rating of Amantra

Amantra Wild Honey Pie

CKCSC, USA, Can. Ch. Amantra Naval Salute

Eng. Ch. Lansola Cornish Settler of Crisdig

Amantra Tippy Canoe

Amantra Tugboat Annie

Can. Ch. Salador Celtic Dirk.

Tricolor Dog
Bred by Shelia Smith, England
Owned by Brigida Reynolds,
Mostyn Cavaliers

Danny was a significant sire in both Canada and the USA. His influence on the breed has been remarkable, as not only his children but his grandchildren have had a far reaching effect on the breed. Some of his get include Reynold's and Hodgkinson's Canadian and AKC Ch, Mostyn Celtic Sorin, Guimond's CKCSC, USA and Canadian Ch. Rutherford Elliot of Shagbark, Phyllis Shortt's Canadian Ch. Mostyn Spencer for Hire and Messrs. Gammon and Schroll's CKCSC, USA Ch. Ravenrush Tartan.

Photo by Alex Smith

Salador Chelsea of Loranka

Eng. Ch. Salador Celtic Prince

Salador Cherrybird

Can Ch. Salador Celtic Dirk

Ronnoc True Love

Eng. Ch. Salador Colleen

Salador Country Girl

Photo by Vavra

CKCSC, USA, Can. Ch. Roydwood Royal Mail.

Blenheim Dog
Bred by Michael Boothroyd, England
Owned by Olivia Darbyshire and Louise Pearce, Mingchen Cavaliers

Top Cavalier in Canada in 1988, BISS winner of the Canadian National and the CKCSC, USA National Specialties in 1989. The second dog to win both National Specialties, and only the second Canadian dog to do so. Sire of Canadian and CKCSC, USA Ch. Laughing Stormin' Norman, CKCSC, USA Reserve National Specialty winner and sire of champions.

Eng. Ch. Leynsord Salutation

Leynsord Tatler

Neville Cream Sherry

CKCSC, USA, Can. Ch. Roydwood Royal Mail

Eng. Ch. Rosemerryn of Alansmere

Roydwood Rock Rose

Roydwood Royal Saphire

Spencer

Can., Ber. Ch. Mostyn Spencer For Hire, Can./ Ber. CDX.

Tricolor Dog
Bred by Brigida Reynolds
Owned by Phyllis Shortt,
Shortbred Cavaliers

Multiple Canadian BISS winner including the 1990 Canadian National Specialty. Top Cavalier in Canada in both Conformation and Obedience in 1991.

Photo by Shortt

Eng. Ch. Salador Celtic Prince

Can. Ch. Salador Celtic Dirk

Eng. Ch. Salador Colleen

Can., Ber. Ch. Mostyn Spencer For Hire, Can./Ber. CDX

Can. Ch. Witsend Puzzle of B.J.

B.J. Vanilla Pudding of Mostyn

Can. Ch. Pattycake of Kindrum & B.J.

Can. Ch. Muffity Fi-Fi.

Blenheim Bitch
Bred by Jenny Hall, England
Owned by Christine Gingell,
Curiadd Cavaliers

Top winning Cavalier bitch in Canada to date, with 2 Canadian BIS wins, Numerous Toy Group Firsts and BISS wins in both Canada and the US.

Photo by Mikron

Muffity Joshua

Muffity My Boy Boris

Muffity Sweet Rose Marie

Can. Ch. Muffity Fi-Fi

Muffity Mystical Magician

Muffity Wizard's Delight

Muffity Jenny's Delight

Can. Ch. Kewpy's Bo Diddley.

Blenheim Dog
Bred and owned by
Karen Wills, Kewpy
Cavaliers

Top winning Canadian Cavalier to date, with 8 Canadian BIS wins as well as BISS wins. More than 50 group firsts. Sire of Canadian Champions and Specialty winners.

Photo by Andy

Can. Ch. Salador Crusader of B.J.

Can. Ch. Glenrobin Hamish of Kewpy

CKCSC, USA, Can. Ch. B.J. Garbo

Can. Ch. Kewpy's Bo Diddley

Caerwen Charisma

Grantilley Tailor Maid

Grantilley Victorian Lady

Photo by Alex Smith

Can., AKC Ch. Happy Boy of Fairytale Forest.

Blenheim Dog
Bred by Harold Magenreuter & Rosemarie Sunkler, Germany
Owned by Dr. Morag Gilchrist, Jean Tremblay and Elaine Mitchell

A Canadian BIS winner, with over 30 BOB wins, and the first Canadian Cavalier to become an AKC Champion.

Geordy du Val Poutrel

Indigo du Val Poutrel

Guerlain du Val Poutrel

Can., AKC Ch. Happy Boy of Fairytale Forest

Can., Ger., Eur. Ch. Grantilley Azario

Grantilley Stormy

Able Princess of Grantilley

Can. & AKC Ch. Mostyn Celtic Sorin

Blenheim Dog
Bred by Brigida Reynolds, Canada
Owned by Brigida Reynolds and
Chris and Shelly Hodgkinson,
Canada

Sorin is a BIS and a BISS winner, as well as the Top Cavalier in Canada for 1997.

Photo by Alex Smith

Eng. Salador Celtic Prince

Can. Ch. Salador Celtic Dirk

Salador Colleen

Can and AKC Ch. Mostyn Celtic Sorin

CKCSC, USA and Can. Ch Laughing Charisma

Mostyn Cherry Sundae

Can. Ch. Mostyn Caroline's Legacy

Lovers in the Park by Francois Boucher. Reproduction courtesy The Putnam Foundation Timkin Museum of Art, San Diego, California.

*C*avaliers in Tapestry

Even before being immortalized on canvas, Cavalier-type spaniels were embroidered into tapestries. "The Offering of the Heart," a magnificent fifteenth-century Arras tapestry that hangs in the Louvre in Paris, has a little spaniel romping in the foreground. In 1836, Queen Victoria's court painter, Sir Edwin Landseer, painted her beloved tricolor "Dash" lying on a velvet footstool, the image of which was eventually transferred onto canvas for Victorian ladies to stitch. The pretty little dogs have been a popular subject for needlepoint enthusiasts ever since.

Antique tapestry pillows.
Owned and photographed by Betty Turner.

Cavaliers in Paintings

Art galleries from east to west contained unexpected surprises, as I discovered in my search for paintings of, or including, Cavaliers.

"Inseparable". Painting by Betty Turner, California.
Reproduction courtesy Betty Turner.

A King Charles Spaniel by Edouard Manet, circa 1866.
Reproduction courtesy The National Gallery of Art, Washington, D.C.

Alexander and Diogenes
by Sir Edwin Landseer.
Reproduction courtesy The Tate Gallery,
London.

Hayley and Midori.
Painting by Tom Lovelace, Texas.
Reproduction courtesy Tom Lovelace.

Cavalier in Afternoon Sun.
Painting by Pamela Dennis Hall,
Texas. Private Collection.

. . 165 . .

Cavaliers in Jewelry

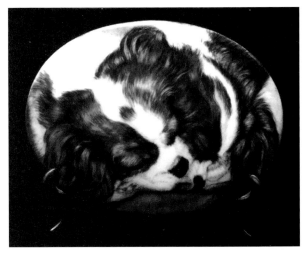

Hand painted porcelain jewelry by Betty Turner, California.
Photo by Turner.

Portraits in Staffordshire

About the time Queen Victoria came to the throne of England in 1837, a generation of potters at "The Potteries" in the English county of Staffordshire began to produce ornamental figures of people and dogs, all of which sold for only a few pennies each.

The majority of the Staffordshire dogs fall into a category known as "comforter spaniels," modeled after King Charles Spaniels of the original type. As many as two hundred different models of these dogs were produced, ranging in size from less than six inches to more than eighteen inches in height. They were made in pairs, generally in one of two forms: those that were meant to be viewed from any angle, and those known as "flatbacks," designed to stand on a mantle shelf. Earlier pairs were more highly colored—copper-tone, gold, chestnut, red, black, and even green—while the later ones were either white or white with rust or black patches. The dogs, which are differently sized to depict male and female, sit on their haunches facing each other, tails wrapped around them. Some are fitted with glass eyes, although eyes are more frequently painted black with a ring of yellow or sometimes blue. Nearly all have chains with a locket at the neck, painted in gold. Most of the dogs have their legs molded to the body with no space between them, while those with open front legs usually are more highly detailed, and of better quality, and are considerably more rare. Some figures have baskets of flowers hanging from their mouths, while others depict dogs with children, especially royal

Staffordshire pieces. Owned and photographed by the author.

children. Kegs, inkwells, spill vases, coin banks, and pitchers were popular, and dogs even adorned clocks with painted-on hands, believed to have been sold to people who could not afford a real mantle clock.

The dogs were so popular that reproductions have been made almost continuously to the present day. Trying to tell whether a Staffordshire figurine is an antique or a counterfeit can be quite difficult, and the unwary can easily mistake a reproduction figure for an original. Weight is important (they should be relatively heavy), as is the patina that ceramics acquire over time. Fine cracks, called crazing, should not be even overall, nor should there be any imprint on the bottom of the piece. Gold should not be too bright, as liquid gold was not used until after the mid 1900s. Small holes should appear in the back or bottom.

In recent years, Victorian Staffordshire figures have become highly collectable. For Cavalier lovers, Staffordshire dogs, either reproduction or original, are a must for their mantle shelves and hearths.

A painted bronze statue. Bronze by Chris Baldwin.

The grass always loooks greener on the other side of the fence.
"Princess" owned by Mr. and Mrs. David Wayham.
Photo by D. Wayham.

tail end

The excellent breeding section of the Code of Ethics of the Cavalier King Charles Spaniel Club, USA, Inc., with which all members have to abide, is reprinted here with permission.

II. Breeding

I realize that the purpose of breeding Cavalier King Charles Spaniels is to attempt to bring their natural qualities to perfection in accordance with the Breed Standard. There exists a constant danger that ignorant or disreputable breeders may, by improper practices, produce physically, mentally or temperamentally unsound specimens to the detriment of the breed. I will consult with the breeder of the dog I own and/or with some other experienced breeder before undertaking any breeding.

A. *If* I decide to breed a litter, I will:

1. To the best of my ability be selective with respect to the conformation, physical well-being, and temperament of the pair to be mated.
2. Breed only after a careful study and understanding of the Breed Standard, as it applies to the pedigrees of the two dogs involved, and to the dogs themselves.
3. Breed only Cavaliers registered with or eligible for registration with the CKCSC.
4. Be prepared to provide the proper care for both the bitch and her litter, and to retain the puppies for as long as is necessary to assure their placement in suitable homes.
5. Never breed from or to any Cavalier known to me to have an inheritable disqualifying, disabling, or potentially disabling defect.
6. Register with CKCSC, in accordance with the Club's Procedures for Registration and Transfer of Dogs, each of my Cavalier litters whelped in the USA.
7. Never breed, or breed to a "Restricted from Breeding Dog or Bitch."

B. As the owner of a stud dog, I realize that I must exercise exemplary conduct in the use of my dog in order to abide by the standards set forth in this Code of Ethics. Therefore I will:

1. Use my dog only on bitches which I feel are an asset to the breed, whose owners agree to conform to this Code of ethics.
2. Supply a duly signed Stud Service Certificate at the time of mating.
3. Be as helpful as possible in assisting the owner of the bitch with the placement of any puppies resulting from the use of my dog, realizing that I am as responsible as the breeder for these puppies.
4. Provide one free return service by the same dog for a bitch which has failed to conceive or to whelp a viable litter as long as the dog is still in my ownership.

C. As the owner of a brood bitch, I realize that I must exercise exemplary conduct in breeding from her in order to abide by the standards set forth in this Code of Ethics. Therefore I will not:

1. Breed a bitch before she is one year old, and then only if she is sufficiently mature

and in excellent health; nor breed a bitch that has reached her eighth birthday.

2. Allow a bitch to whelp more than tw litters during any three consecutive seasons.

3. Allow a bitch to carry to term and rear more than six litters in her lifetime.

III. Care And Transfer of Puppies And Dogs

A. I will provide all puppies with proper veterinary and home care, which includes:

1. Checking into the removal of dewclaws, including hind dewclaws if present. The CKCSC strongly recommends the removal of front dewclaws to prevent the eyes from being damaged.

2. The elimination of parasites, internal and external.

3. The necessary inoculations.

4. A properly balanced nutritional diet as recommended by the veterinarian.

B. I will ask my veterinarian to euthanise any puppy found to be deformed or suffering from an irreversible illness.

C. I will do my best to evaluate my Cavaliers objectively and to use for breeding only those conforming closely to the Breed Standard. All others I will either have neutered before transferring them, or will transfer with a CKCSC "Restricted Transfer of Dog" form, duty signed by buyer and seller, restricting the Cavalier from being used for breeding purposes.

D. I will to the very best of my ability screen all prospective new owners to determine their suitability and their motives in acquiring a Cavalier. Special attention will be given to the necessary commitment to financial responsibility for proper care and adequate physical facilities.

E. I will not allow any puppy to leave for its new home before the age of eight weeks. The CKCSC

recommends ten to twelve weeks as the appropriate age for transfer.

F. I will make sure that each of my Cavaliers, upon being released to its new owner, is accompanied by the following:

1. Feeding instructions.

2. Written medical records, which will include immunizations, types of vaccines used, date(s) of inoculations, date(s) of worming it any.

3. A pedigree showing at least three generations.

4. A copy of this Code of Ethics.

5. A CKCSC New Membership Application form.

6. A Certificate of Health, signed by my veterinarian.

G. I will see that the necessary forms and fees to transfer ownership are submitted to the Registration Secretary.

H. I will encourage all new owners to have their Cavaliers checked by a veterinarian within forty-eight hours of time of acquisition.

I. I will encourage all new owners to keep me informed concerning the development of any Cavalier obtained from me, and to advise me of any problems that may develop during its lifetime, as well as of the eventual cause of death.

J. I will ask the owner(s) of any dog acquired from me to advise me if they are ever unable to keep their Cavalier, so that I can either take the dog back or give every assistance in re-homing it.

K. I understand that if I co-own a dog it is wise to have a contract drawn up, signed by both co-owners, stating the exact terms of co-ownership.

L. I will be certain that any advertising I do of my Cavaliers, written or oral, is factual and honest in both substance and implication.

Clubs and Organizations

- *The Cavalier King Charles Spaniel Club, USA, Inc.*
  Denise Quittmeyer, Membership Chairman
  2630 South Buffalo Drive
  Las Vegas, NV 89117-2916 USA

  Regional Clubs of the CKCSC, USA, Inc.
      Cavaliers of the West
      Cavaliers of the Mid-West
      Cavaliers of the South
      Cavaliers of the North East

- *The American Kennel Club*
  51 Madison Ave.
  New York, NY 10010 USA

- *The American Cavalier King Charles Spaniel Club*
  Kathy Caplan, Membership Chairman
  1018 Scotts Hill Dr.
  Baltimore, MD 21208   USA

- *The Canadian Kennel Club*
  100-89 Skyway Ave.
  Etobicoke, Ontario M9W 6R4   CANADA

- *The Cavalier King Charles Spaniel Club of Canada*
  Frances Bowness, Secretary
  860 Anderson Ave
  Milton, Ontario L9T 4X8 CANADA

  Regional Clubs of the CKCSCC
    Cavalier Fanciers of Southern Ontario
    Cavalier King Charles Spaniels of
      British Columbia
    Cavalier King Charles Spaniels of
      Mid-Western Canada

- *The Cavalier King Charles Spaniel Club (England)*
  Mrs. Lesley Jupp, Secretary
  60 Roundway, Copped Hall
  Camberley, Surrey, England

Books of Interest

Cavalier King Charles Spaniels

- All About the Cavalier King Charles Spaniel by Evelyn Booth, 1983 Pelham Books, England.
- The Royal Toy Spaniels by Alicia Pennington. 1989 Ringpress Books, England.
- The Cavalier King Charles Spaniel, An Owner's Companion by John Evans, England. 1990 Howell Books USA.
- The Cavalier King Charles Spaniel by Bruce Field. 1995 Robert Hale Ltd., England.
- Cavalier King Charles Spaniels Today by Sheila Smith, England. 1995 Howell Book House, USA.

Magazines and Periodicals

- The Royal Spaniels
  14531 Jefferson St.,
  Midway City, CA 92655
- The Bulletin of the CKCSC, USA
- The AKC Gazette
- Dogs in Canada
- Love of Animals- Natural Health Care and Healing
  7811 Montrose Rd.,
  P.O. Box 60042, Montrose, MD 20859-0042

Deafness

- Living With a Deaf Dog,
  Susan Cope Becker, USA

Reproduction

- Canine Reproduction, a Breeder's Guide by Phyllis A. Holst, MS, DVM. 1985, Alpine Blue Ribbon Books, USA

Movement

- The Dog in Action,
  by McDowell Lyon.
  1950 Howell Book House, USA

- Structure and Terminology,
  by Gilbert and Brown.
  1995 Howell Book House, USA

Alternative Foods

- Reigning Cats and Dogs
  by Pat MacKay, USA

Health Information

- Hip and Elbow Certification
  OFA (Orthopedic Foundation for Animals)
    Dr. E. Corley
    2300 Nifong Blvd.
    Columbia, MO 65201   USA
  Penn Hip
    c/o International Canine Genetics
    271 Great Valley Parkway
    Malvern, PA 19335   USA
- Eye Certification
  CERF (Canine Eye Registration Foundation)
    SCCA, Purdue University
    1235 SCC-A
    W. Lafayette, IN 47907   USA

- Thyroid Testing
  Michigan State University
  Animal Health Diagnostic Laboratory
  P.O. Box 30076
  Lansing, MI 48909   USA
  517-353-1683
- Canine Blood Bank
  Hemopet
  938 Stanford St.
  Santa Monica, CA 90403   USA
- Heart Studies
  University of Pennsylvania
    Dr. James Buchanan,
    Dept. Veterinary Cardiology
    Philadelphia, PA 19104   USA
  The University of Guelph
    Dr. Michael O'Grady
    Dept. Veterinary Cardiology
    3850 Spruce St.
    Guelph, Ontario   CANADA

The perfect dog, is one that even mows the yard. A Royal Companion Cavalier, owned by Windy Hilburts-Goodman. Photo by Dalton.

Tribute to a Dog

"The one absolutely unselfish friend that man can have in this world, the one that never deserts him, the one that never proves ungrateful or treacherous, is his dog. A man's dog stands by him in prosperity and in poverty, in health and in sickness. He will sleep on the cold ground, where the wintery winds blow and the snow drives fiercely, if only he may be near his master's side. He will kiss the hand that has no food to offer; he will lick the wounds and sores that come in encounter with the roughness of the world. He guards the sleep of his pauper master as if he were a prince. When all other friends desert, he remains. When riches take wings and reputation falls to pieces, he is constant in his love as the sun in its journey through the heavens."

Senator George Vest, 1870

Serenity.
Photo by Vicki Roach.

glossary

EXPLANATION OF COMMON TERMS USED IN CRITIQUES

*F*or a detailed explanation and understanding of canine structure and terminology, rcad K-9 Structure & Terminology by Brown and The Dog in Action by McDowell Lyon.

Angulation
Front: The angle formed by the bones of the shoulder blade and upper arm.
Rear: The angle formed between the upper and lower thigh. The angle formed by the lower thigh and hock.

Balanced Everything correctly proportioned.

Bitchy Femine male.

Bodied up Mature and well developed, including spring of rib.

Coarse Overdone or heavy, too much bone.

Cobby compact, short bodied.

Cow hocked Hocks turn inward towards each other.

Crabbing Forward movement at an angle to straight ahead. Not tracking properly.

Crossing over When one leg crosses in front of the other when moving.

Doggy Masculine bitch.

Down faced Line of top of muzzle tips downwards.

Down in pastern Sloping pastern.

Ear leather Ear flap, excluding hair.

Elbows, out Not held tightly to body, rotating outwards.

Elbows, tied in Elbows so close to body, dog has no reach.

Expression Facial communication. Melting expression: heart rending, sweet;
Foreign expression: Un-Cavalier, mean.

Feet, East West Feet turn outwards.

Fill beneath the eyes Padding on muzzle or cushioning beneath eyes.

Front, Chippendale Crooked legs.

Front, straight Legs parallel to each other when viewed from front (correct).

Furnishings Fringes on ears, legs, tail, undercarriage, pants.

Hackney action Lifting front legs up instead of reaching forward and covering ground.

Hocks, cow Hocks turn toward each other.

Hocks, high in Long hocks, or too much distance from tip of hock to ground.

Hocks, well let down Short hocks (correct).

Hocks, sickle No flexibility of hock.

Hyper-extended hock Hock joint buckles forward, causing hock to bow.

Jowls Loose skin of mouth and/or throat.

Knuckling-over Pastern joint bends forward.

Layback Shoulder blade angle: ideally, but rarely 45 degrees.

Leggy Legs too long.

Lips, pendulous Droopy, like bloodhound.

Lips, tight and clean Lips fit muzzle without droop.

Long cast Long in loin, not cobby.

Moving close behind Legs too close together when moving.

Moving with drive At the trot the hock is well flexed and reaches well under the dog. Not sickle hocked.

Neck, reach of Neck correctly proportioned, neither too long nor too short.

Neck, well set on Neck flows smoothly and gracefully into shoulders.

Stuffy neck Neck too short.

Nose, butterfly White flesh marks on nose.

Nose, Dudley Nose off-color, gray or brownish, not black.
Outline Silhouette.

Pace Both front and rear legs move forward in tandem.

Paddling Front legs move with a circular motion.

Particolors Blenheims and tricolors.

Pigeon-toed Front feet face each other.

Pigment Color of nose, eyerims and lips.

Proud tail High tail carriage.

Rangy Long in loin.

Ribs, well sprung Ribs neither flat nor too rounded.

Roach Back arched.

Short-coupled Short loin.

Shoulders, loaded Too much muscle.

Shoulders, straight Incorrect angulation.

Slab-sided Ribs flat, lack of spring.

Snipey Pointed muzzle, no fill or padding.

Sound Correct structure and disposition, healthy.

Square Height at withers same as length of body.

Stacking Setting up.

Straight stifle Lacking angulation. Stifle not properly bent.

Substance Good bone and muscle developement.

Throatiness Too much loose skin under throat.

Topline Line of back.

Tuck-up Greyhound look. Bottom line angles up to waist.

Up on leg Legs too long in proportion to depth of body; leggy.

Up to size As big as one would want.

Weedy Lacking bone and body.

Well broken On particolors, color well interspersed with white.

Whole colors Black and tans and rubys.

Patience

This drawing of a Cavalier family has been accepted for exhibition at the 1998 Art Show at the Dog Show, in an unprecedented entry of nearly seven hundred. The artist, Miss Michael Allen, is America's most published show dog artist in America today and her works have graced the covers of publications in Japan, Hong Kong, Taiwan, Finland, France and Australia as well as America. Miss Allen is the editor and publisher of The Royal Spaniels, award winning magazine devoted to King Charles Spaniels. She resides in Midway City, California.